Alexander MEN

A WITNESS FOR
CONTEMPORARY RUSSIA
A Man for Our Times

Acts of Faith

Acts of Faith

In his last lecture, given the night before his assasination in 1990, Fr. Alexander Men spoke on the simple theme, which in the end was the theme of his entire life, of "Christianity." The tone of his words was, as always, bold and confident. "The victory which begins on the night of the Resurrection," he states, "will continue as long as the world exists."

The renewal of Christianity in Russia today, the virtual rebaptism of the nation, exemplifies that power of resurrection and is surely one of the most remarkable events in our time. This renewal, and all the changes in Russia, cannot be understood without understanding the life and work of Fr. Alexander Men. Perhaps more than anyone else, it was Fr. Men who—as the physicist Alexei Tsvelik says—showed a society accustomed to living in fear the way to living without fear. This absolute fearlessness was no doubt due to his complex God-centeredness. "God must be not only first in life," he would say in a tone his hearers remember as ringing and joyous, "he must be All in all!"

So Yves Hamant's vivid and brilliant biography of this vibrant figure must be welcome to anyone interested in Russia and the dramatic changes which are taking place there. However it seems to me that this man, Fr. Men, whose works are only beginning to be made available in English, has a message of incalcuable importance for Christians in America as well. By his example of courage and of embracing other Christians without discrimination—"our walls of division do not rise to heaven" he would say—together with his confident engaging in dialogue with unbelivers and even enemies of Christianity, does he not give an example for Christians here who, let us admit it, are too often isolated, divided and fearful before the currents of our time? Also, with an incomparable clarity, which Hamant's work reflects so well, he recalls us to the "one thing needful"—to that living heart of what religion is all about, yesterday, today and tomorrow, the love of God and the eternal victory of the Resurrection.

Thus the life of Fr. Alexander Men and his teaching are not only of historical importance to the nation of Russia, though they certainly are that, but also they are a gift, and a challenge, and a way forward for us in the West as well. For this reason the publication of this biography, and of the works of Fr. Men himself which will follow from Oakwood Publications, seems to us to be an event of the greatest significance; to be that rarest of literary effort which calls forth joy and thankfulness of heart.

Seraphim Joseph Sigrist
Orthodox Bishop, formerly of Sendai and East Japan

On September 9, 1990, near Moscow, an Orthodox priest was attacked and killed by someone wielding an axe. The death of this priest, Fr. Alexander Men, revealed his personality to the world. Through his increasing spiritual influence, Fr. Alexander was beginning to fill the space left empty by the death of Sakharov.

He was baptized by a priest of the Catacomb Church during the worst period of Stalin's persecutions; he was encouraged in his vocation by the priest who had baptized Stalin's daughter; he was closely linked to Frs. Yakunin and Dudko, was a friend of Solzhenitsyn, and was regularly harrassed by the KGB; and he experienced first hand the events that his country lived through during the 50 years preceding his death.

By setting Fr. Alexander's life and activity in their historical context, this book tells the story of a very exceptional figure.

THE PROPHET EZEKIEL. PAINTED BY FR. ALEXANDER MEN (1950)

Having completed advanced studies in Russian and a doctorate in political science, Yves Hamant teaches Russian civilization at the University of Paris X-Nanterre. He lived for years in Russia during the Brezhnev period. In his memoirs, Solzhenitsyn has this to say about Yves Hamant: "He was very much in love with Russian culture and helped us a great deal at that time." Having known Fr. Alexander personally since 1970, the author is a member of the commission created by the Patriarchate of Moscow to preserve and make known Fr. Alexander's works.

Fr. Steven Bigham is a scholar and researcher of Orthodox tradition (The Image of God the Father in Orthodox Theology and Iconography and Other Studies) and a translator of several previous Oakwood publications (The Icon: Image of the Invisible; The Art of the Icon; The Ministry of Women in the Church; The Place of the Heart). A graduate of St. Vladimir's Seminary in New York, he holds a doctorate from the University of Montreal in theology with a specialization in Christian and Orthodox iconography.

Reflections of a Friend

The book which you are holding in your hands, dear reader, not only tells about a singularly brilliant individual, the priest Fr. Alexander Men', but also about a very important side of the life of Russia, which can aptly be called the interrelationship of the Church and the state.

Inasmuch as communist Russia represented itself as a country in which ideology was given first place, the way in which the state related to religion and the Church became one of the more important indicators of the inner workings of the whole system. This state-Church relationship took on different shapes in the regimes of Stalin, Khrushchev, Brezhnev and Gorbachav. The book clearly links the personal development of the future priest and his later pastoral labours with the changing sociopolitical background. It highlights the constant interaction of two opposing forces: on one side, there is the eternal search for God's truth and selfless service for the sake of this truth, and on the other, resistance to this truth from "this world."

Fr. Alexander Men' lived the life of the Orthodox Church from the very moment of his birth. He was molded and formed under the unfailing influence of an ecclesiastical milieu marked by depth, intelligence, and an openness to the needs of the world, and which represented the continuation of the spiritual tradition of the Optina Elders and the famous Moscow priest Fr. Aleksey Mechev.

The openness of this Orthodox Christian position was not inherited from the dissident circles of the intelligensia of the 1960's. It came rather from the depths of the life of the Church, which was forced to remain in the background for many years because of fierce opposition from the atheistic dictatorship, which used all means available to the state in an effort to remove all spiritual content from daily life.

It is precisely this atheistic opposition that helped form Fr. Alexander's ability to choose the most essential themes for sermons, conversations, and books about the faith, the Bible, and spiritual life, which furthered the author's efforts to spread the gospel to many homes in which there was a great thirst for the truth about the faith. In the words of our celebrated philologist S. S. Averintsev, the *ascesis* of Fr. Alexander Men' can be found partly in the fact that he gathered material for his books about the history of Biblical revelation under conditions in which everything was done by the state to ensure that such books did not appear. He made the impossible possible.

Even more surprising is the rare combination which we find in Fr. Alexander Men's person of an insightful academic researcher and prolific writer and a wise and gentle shepherd of the Orthodox Church. Usually an academic, having surrounded himself with volumes of books, does not show any particular ability or desire for pastoral contact with parishioners. Nor is a pastorally inclined priest usually an accomplished scholar. In Fr. Alexander's personality, both aspirations were combined: the desire to have a greater and deeper knowledge of sacred Scripture, history, and theology, and the desire to communicate the essence of this knowledge to as many people as possible.

Fr. Alexander Men' will be a constant example and reminder of how much a person can do in conditions where everything is directed against him, and of how much unexploited potential there is in every person. The last three years of Fr. Alexander Men's life were truly years of triumph for this celebrated preacher in conditions of freedom which had finally arrived. For it will always remain an enigma why the omnipotent God permitted the martyrdom of his wonderful servant: a servant who had been formed in the bleak years of Stalin's rule; who had lived through the years of Khruschev's persecution of the church; who had then started his brilliant literary work, which came into full bloom in the stagnant Brezhnev years; and who, in the end, was taken from this world on the eve of the downfall of the entire Soviet System, the disintegration of the Soviet Union, and the dawning of a completely new era in the life of Russia.

Perhaps God gave us this wonderful servant to encourage us in the most trying time, and now by his martyrdom is calling us to carry on without him to bring about in our lives a Christianity that is open to the world, the kind for which Fr. Alexander Men' worked, following in the footsteps of the best pastors of the Russian Orthodox Church.

In conclusion, I would like to cite the words of a foreigner who lived in Russia for several years and later, having read Yves Hamant's book about Fr. Alexander Men', said, "I discovered more about the life of the Russian Orthodox Church from this book than from living in Russia for three years."

Fr. Alexander Borisov. Pastor,
Church of the Holy Unmercenaries,
Cosmas and Damian, Moscow

President, Bible Society in Russia

Translated by Fr. Maxym Lysack

Alexander MEN:

A Witness for Contemporary Russia
(*A Man For Our Times*)

Yves Hamant

Translation by Fr. Steven Bigham
Introduction by Fr. Maxym Lysack

Oakwood Publications

Originally Published in French under the title:
Alexandre MEN: Un Temoin Pour La Russie de Ce Temps
by Editions MAME, Paris 1993

Copyright © 1995 Oakwood Publications [English Edition]

Published by: Oakwood Publications
                     3827 Bluff St.
                Torrance, California 90505-6359

ISBN No. 1-879038-12-9

Typesetting: Peninsula Pointe Services, Torrance, CA
               Victoria Graphics, Orange, CA
Proofreading and Editing: Michael Bonketoff
Cover: Victoria Graphics, Orange, CA
Printed in the U.S.A. by KNI, Inc., Anaheim, CA

Table of Contents

FR. ALEXANDER MEN'S GRAVE (CLOSE-UP)

FR. MAXYM LYSACK AT THE GRAVE OF FR. MEN

FR. ALEXANDER MEN'S LAST PARISH (MEETING OF THE LORD)*. GRAVE IS TO THE LEFT OF THIS CHURCH. *NOVAYA DEREVNYA (PUSHKINO)

MARKER AT THE SPOT WHERE FR. ALEXANDER WAS MARTYRED (MAY 1993)

FR. ALEXANDER'S HOUSE IN SEMKHOZ

Introduction to the English-Language Edition

And his gifts were that some should be apostles, some prophets, some evangelists, some pastors and teachers, to equip the saints for the work of ministry, for the building up of the body of Christ.... (Ephesians 4:11-12)

In these verses from his Epistle to the Ephesians, St. Paul presents five essential ministries given to the Church for its edification. In his own life, Fr. Alexander Men' manifested aspects of all five of these ministries. As an evangelist, pastor and teacher, most especially, Fr. Alexander shone with the radiance peculiar to those who have a deep sense of vocation and have given themselves over entirely to their calling.

Fr. Alexander was a highly gifted individual; more specifically, he had many natural talents, which he honed to a high degree of perfection, and he was himself a gift to the Church in the ministries God gave him. It is of course this latter type of gifting that Saint Paul had in mind. God did not give ministries to the Church in a purely theoretical sense; rather, He made them real in obedient individuals. The actual gifts, then, are Christians who submit themselves to the calling God gives them and persevere in their vocations. Over a period of many years, Fr. Alexander patiently and lovingly laboured for the edification of Christ's Church and in particular for the Russian Orthodox Church, which he loved so much.

Fr. Alexander was, in many ways, an apostle to the generations of new believers that emerged in the Soviet Union in the 60s, 70s and 80s. In the Orthodox tradition, the ministry of apostle is often equated with the office of bishop. In a general sense, however, an apostle is any man or woman sent bearing the gospel to a specific people. Among the saints there are many who are considered equal to the apostles for their witness to Christ in their generation. An apostle has a strong sense of vocation precisely because he knows he is sent to accomplish a particular task. Yves Hamant so vividly presents Fr. Men's strong sense of calling on his own life. We are told of how single-minded he was in his vocation. We see how Fr. Alexander's calling was formed and nurtured through the conversion of his mother and aunt. This calling was doubtless brought into focus in the context of the underground Church in the crucible of persecution. Fr. Alexander never lost sight of his apostolic calling, even to the last moments of his life. He knew not only what his calling was, but also the One who had called him. It was Fr. Alexander's personal relationship with Christ that was displayed in the joy and energy with which he pursued his vocation.

Fr. Alexander's prophetic ministry was directed primarily toward two constituencies: Soviet society and the Russian Orthodox Church. He was well equipped to address the emptiness in Soviet society. He knew all of its weaknesses and wounds. With great skill he could demonstrate the irrational and unscientific basis of "scientific atheism." In addition, Fr. Alexander's great interest in and acquaintance with literature and the arts enabled him to dialogue with his contemporary culture in a profound way. He could speak to every aspect of Soviet society with an appreciation for its sins as well as its potential. Hamant shows Fr. Alexander to be a man of great hope who, even in the darkest times, could see Christ pulling Soviet culture toward an eventual catharsis and conversion.

Fr. Alexander knew that a time of crisis in Soviet society was on its way. His life, vocation, research and writing prepared him for the moment when the Church would be set free. Here Fr. Alexander was able to speak prophetically to his own Church:

> "The most difficult time for the Church will come when everything is permitted. Then we will be ashamed because we are not ready to bear witness, and unfortunately we are preparing ourselves very poorly for that moment."[1]

Once the complete collapse of communism became evident, many began to look to the Russian Orthodox Church to fill the spiritual and moral void left in Soviet society and culture. Russian Orthodox parishes were inundated with people seeking baptism. Fr. Alexander continued to emphasize the urgency of spiritually restoring the people. At a time when many churches and monasteries were being returned to the Church by the government, the temptation for the Church was to focus its time, energy and resources on the restoration of buildings, thus unintentionally neglecting the spiritual needs of the faithful. Christ had not called the Church to be the custodian of religious material culture, but to be light and salt in a world desperately hungry for transformation in Christ. Fr. Alexander challenged the Church to fulfil its mandate. He exercised this prophetic ministry in a spirit of love. Even if he occasionally expressed disappointment in it, there was nothing rebellious in how Fr. Alexander related to his Church, nor was there any bitterness. In fact, he had a great respect for his bishops and a good relationship with his local bishop, Metropolitan Juvenaly.

For many years of his pastoral ministry, Fr. Alexander could not work too openly as an evangelist. Rather, he carried out his work on a small scale by preaching and teaching in his parish church. He also accomplished much of his evangelistic work one-to-one. His third method of evangelism was through his books, which he likened to arrows shot from a bow: they kept flying (being read and exerting an influence) long after they had been fired (written and published). At last, however, Fr. Alexander took his place as an evangelist working on a larger scale. In his own words, he was doing the same things he had always done but simply with larger groups. He found himself addressing crowds in auditoria and, for a very short time before his death, over television. Many in Russian society must have been surprised at Fr. Alexander's "sudden entry" onto the national scene. However, as Hamant points out, there was nothing "sudden" about it. Fr. Alexander had spent his whole priestly ministry as an evangelist patiently awaiting the time when there would be a demand for him to operate in the open.

Among the five ministry gifts listed in the book of Ephesians, two are normally joined together to reflect two aspects of the same office. These are the ministries of pastor and teacher. The two ministries were most commonly combined in the office of presbyter in the early Church. In Fr. Alexander, we discover the image of a true Orthodox pastor. He was well known for his great commitment to his spiritual children and for his personal availability to them. Yves Hamant has written in effect a theology of pastoral care simply by describing the pastoral *modus operandi* of Fr. Alexander. Here we see that the relationship between the pastor and the spiritual child is personal and intense while being at the same time respectful and uncontrolling. There is an emphasis on frequent confession. The priest enables his spiritual child to choose, but does not choose for him.

In Fr. Alexander we also find the humility so indispensable to any pastor. What might be described as an awareness of one's limits of competence is found in his belief in the qualitative difference between two types of pastoral relationships: the one between a parishioner and a spiritual father in the parish context, and the other between a *starets* (elder) and spiritual child in the monastic context. *Starchestvo*, or eldership, is not given automatically through ordination to the priesthood. This particular ministry is given to a few, and not always to priests, with time and maturity. Fr. Alexander believed that every parish priest needed to minister in a way consistent with his context. While not necessarily a *starets*, every parish priest is called to provide personal, loving pastoral guidance to all who approach him.

In Fr. Alexander's priestly ministry, pastoring and teaching were inseparable. As a teacher, he exercised a great pastoral sensitivity, whether he was preparing catechumens for baptism, speaking to a large audience, or writing; in all of these situations, as Archbishop Mikhail points out in the Foreword, Fr. Alexander was careful to use contemporary language and concepts that would be understood by all. Furthermore, through his powerful teaching charism, he was able to render the most difficult theological principles comprehensible to his hearers. Hamant describes how Fr. Alexander could relate on an individual basis to different people in an audience when speaking in public. Every question became a pastoral door for him. His strong pastoral presence, full of love and vitality, gave his teaching the quality of a personal encounter rather than of a dry didactic exercise.

An important part of Fr. Alexander's great pastoral gift was his ability clearly to articulate a very real interior life. His transparency and genuineness operated as magnets drawing many spiritual children. Among them can be found monastics, parish priests, scientists, artists, performers, *babushky*, writers, politicians -- indeed, individuals from all walks of life.

When I visited Moscow in May of 1993 at the invitation of some of Fr. Alexander's spiritual children, I was struck by the sheer number and variety of people who had been strongly influenced by him. Among the priests I would need to mention Fr. Alexander Borisov, pastor of SS. Cosmas and Damian parish in Moscow and a long-standing friend of Fr. Alexander's. His parish is a veritable centre of missionary activity and incorporates many of the ideals that Fr. Men' embraced. Fr. Ignatiy Krekshin, a spiritual son of Fr. Alexander's, is the *igumen* (abbot) of a new monastic community. He is a specialist in the area of biblical studies and includes teaching and missionary work as part of his monastic vocation. He contributed the Preface to this edition. Both priests are typical of the many clergy who were in some way associated with Fr. Alexander: all of them are exemplary pastors who exhibit a true missionary spirit. They remain loyal to the Russian Orthodox Church while maintaining a characteristic openness to dialogue and co-operation with other Christians where possible. Many of the lay people who are spiritual children of Fr. Alexander's are active in lay fellowships (traditionally called brotherhoods in the Orthodox Church) oriented to catechetical and evangelistic work. They are deeply committed to work among the poor and to the task of reconciliation among Christians.

Fr. Alexander's death was a tragedy for Russia. As one watches the spiritual situation in Russia as it passes through a period of upheaval in every area, one cannot help but wonder about the contribution such a gifted and faithful pastor might have made to its further spiritual development. Nevertheless, a basic biblical principle gives us pause:

Truly, truly, I say to you, unless a grain of wheat falls into the earth and dies, it remains alone; but if it dies, it bears much fruit. (John 12:24)

Russia and the Orthodox Church have lost a great shepherd but gained a great martyr. Fr. Alexander's martyrdom has become a wellspring of spiritual renewal. It has borne fruit in the diverse ministries of his spiritual children, in his books (new "arrows" are being launched all the time, while the old ones continue to fly) and in the many people who will yet be drawn to Christ through the quality of his witness ("martyr" means "witness" in Greek) in both life and death.

Fr. Maxym Lysack, Pastor,
Christ the Saviour Orthodox Mission
Ottowa, Canada
(Orthodox Chaplain, University of Ottowa)

Foreword[2]

Father Alexander Men' was a man whose personality manifested itself with extraordinary power and brilliance both in his relationships and in the legacy of his works. It is precisely through this legacy that I developed my first impression of him as a wonderful Christian and theologian and a committed struggler for the cause of Christ. Such a man he was, and lives on to be, both in his works and in the memory of those who had the good fortune to know him personally.

I remember with what delight I held in my hands *Sources of Religion*, his second book to be printed abroad. (Of course, the publication of literature of this type at home was impossible for us at that time.) I thought to myself that this was exactly what was needed first and foremost: spiritual food destined for the members of our society, who had been raised in atheism and alienated from any kind of religious tradition. A book like this had a tremendous impact on those who did not believe and those hesitant to believe.

I myself was a witness of how my brother, a man of great culture, an engineer and amateur singer, having read *Sources of Religion* exclaimed: "What exceptional erudition! How well-read the author must be to express his views with such convincing argumentation, and to draw from such rich material!" I will not even speak of the courage that was needed then to decide to publish one's works abroad when so few as yet dared to do this because of the danger it posed for them.

Then the book *Son of Man* fell into our hands, although it had appeared earlier. This book can be given to anyone and he will read it with interest. In the case of an unbelieving person, it will change his way of relating to faith. This does not mean that he will necessarily turn to God, but the book will enhance his idea of the Christian life, of its holiness and majesty -- the majesty of Christ Himself. In this way, it clears the way and prepares the ground for the person's conversion to God.

All of his knowledge, encyclopedic erudition, his most diverse interests in science, *belles lettres* and art, all the talents which God had given him, Fr. Alexander consecrated to preaching. He preached ceaselessly. On point of principle, he always preached in a language accessible to his contemporaries.

I think that Christ Himself gave us direct instruction on how to speak with people. He told His disciples: "To you it has been given to know the secrets of the Kingdom of God; but for others they are in parables...." (Luke 8:10). Now by this yearning of the Saviour to adapt Himself to the level of people's understanding and to their spiritual questions and abilities, we ought to be inspired to imitate Him. In other words, we need to address people in such a way that they understand us, in such a way that our words cause them to take a salutary direction -- in other words, to further their spiritual development, their drawing near to God and, finally, their salvation. Fr. Alexander's work was oriented in exactly this direction.

He understood very well that the mind, not just the will, needed to play a role here in this process. In the parable of the sower we are told how some seed, that is to say preaching, is lost because it has not been grasped with understanding. The devil comes and removes it, that is, he abducts the word which has been heard but not assimilated by the mind (Matthew 13:19). It is not enough simply to induce feelings of piety and rapture; it is not enough to have good will only; a Christian ought to press on towards God with all his soul's strength and, it goes without saying, with his mind as well. (By "mind" here should be understood above all the contemplation and assimilation of the Word of God.)

The Saviour preached in a language familiar to his listeners and made use of images within their grasp. And His explanations never posed any barriers to the assimilation of the truth He proclaimed.

Not by accident did Fr. Alexander devote his first book *Son of Man* to the divine-human person of Jesus Christ. It was Christ whom Fr. Alexander had as the cornerstone of his ministry and writing. One is impressed first and foremost with the christological character of his writings. All of his works (even when he was not touching on Christian teaching directly -- for example, when he wrote about ancient religions) were permeated with the christocentric mindset of the author and by his understanding of religious and confessional diversity as being bathed in the rays of the light of Christ, Who lived in his soul, working graciously upon his readers, and in his life, on his listeners. One would think that never far from his sight were the words of the Apostle: "For no other foundation can anyone lay than that which is laid, which is Jesus Christ" (1 Corinthians 3:11). All his pastoral practice was subordinated to one goal: to lead souls to a personal encounter with Christ the Saviour, and to inculcate in them love towards Christ.

After all, the first commandment says: "...you shall love the Lord your God with all your heart, and with all your soul, and with all your mind, and with all your strength" (Mark 12:30).

But it was difficult for people to love God. And Christ came to earth and became man so that, in loving Christ as a person close to all of us, we would love the heavenly Father, since the Son of God and the Father are one. Unfortunately, although we call ourselves Christians, that love is often found wanting in us. Many worshippers concentrate on the sights and sounds of the rite of prayer, replacing the saving Word of God with various types of graceless verbal exercises, that is to say, "...teaching as doctrines the precepts of men" (Matthew 15:9). In such cases, Christ and His words are not infrequently relegated to the outer reaches of one's awareness instead of occupying in it a commanding position. Fr. Alexander tried with all of his strength to awaken in people, including his parishioners and spiritual children, genuine love towards Christ, and it is precisely for this reason that his ministry was so fruitful.

I became acquainted personally with Fr. Alexander several years before his death. He used to come to Vologda, where I was then the ruling bishop, and stay with me. We had time for friendly fellowship. Later we used to meet in Moscow.

This was a man of uncommon spirituality who led an ascetical life and finished it as a martyr. But in the blood of martyrs, as is known from ancient times, sprout the seeds of the Christian Gospel, and the Church of Christ grows and is strengthened.

Many reproach Fr. Alexander for not conforming sufficiently to certain conventions of Orthodox churchmanship, although in his own pastoral work he did not depart from established liturgical practice and, in this fashion, he in no way opposed the customs and habits of any Orthodox worshipper. However, all who entered into personal contact with him, and even more so, experienced his liturgical celebrations, sensed the inner freedom of his prayerful communion with the heavenly Father, a freedom filled with the Spirit, Who, according to the words of the Saviour, "blows where it wills" (John 3:8). It is precisely this inner freedom which was, perhaps, one of the most distinctive features of his mentality, which made his ministry, preaching and his entire personality so attractive.

Fr. Alexander was indeed a prophet of a new era and a herald of the evangelization of the entire ministry of the Orthodox Church,[3] an evangelization which meets the urgent needs and expectations of the Orthodox people.

Archbishop MIKHAIL (Mudyugin)

(translated by Fr. Maxym Lysack)

Preface

In his Epistle to the Romans, the holy apostle Paul writes fervently about the salvific mission of the preacher, who proclaims the mystery of God to the world:

> For 'every one who calls upon the name of the Lord will be saved.' But how are men to call upon him in whom they have not believed? And how are they to believe in him of whom they have never heard? And how are they to hear without a preacher? And how can men preach unless they are sent?
>
> (Romans 10:13-15a)

And it is precisely through preaching that faith is born:

> So faith comes from what is heard, and what is heard comes by the preaching of Christ.
>
> (Romans 10:17)

From the earliest days of Church history, the apostolic and missionary ministry was entrusted by Christ Himself to every Christian and, most especially, to every priest:

> Go therefore and make disciples of all nations, baptizing them in the name of the Father and of the Son and of the Holy Spirit.
>
> (Matthew 28:19)

Fr. Alexander Men' seriously and courageously treated the mission with which he had been entrusted right from the beginning of his own ministry, when this mission was called "religious propaganda" and was counted as a punishable crime. I remember how, half joking, he spoke to me about the marginal position of the clergy in society: "We priests are considered third-rate citizens, pariahs. How are we really any different from convicts?" When, however, was the preaching of the Kingdom ever comfortable for the world? Hardly in our own evil time!

The sobriety of Fr. Alexander's ministry or, in the words of Dietrich Bonhoeffer, his "sense of responsibility for the faith," consisted in addressing his preaching to real people and in his ability to find the exact word for the proclamation of the Gospel in the contemporary world, a world not distiguished by its "adequacy,"[4] without profaning the exalted nature of the Gospel message.

A stranger to the pseudo-Byzantine rhetorical style of sermon, which transforms preaching into a cold didactic formula, Fr. Alexander returned to the early Christian *kerygma*, which radically changed the world. Although the Russian scholar and religious thinker Sergey Averintsev, in his obituary of Fr. Alexander, called him a missionary to the members of the intelligentsia (it is well known in Russia how much work is involved in this particular mission field), Fr. Alexander's preaching was directed not only to the intelligentsia, but to all manner of people.

I remember how, in the mid-eighties, after a Sunday sermon in one of the Moscow parishes, one of those "typical" old women, the kind who to this day still fill our churches, approached me and said, "The sermon today was wonderful, but the likes of the sermons preached by that priest Men' from Pushkino you will not hear."

The particularity of Fr. Men's theological works can be found in their orientation toward the contemporary person. The last thing he would have considered himself was an academic theologian, although in fact he had a truly encyclopedic knowledge—one need only peruse the bibliography accompanying his apologetical works to be convinced of this. In conversation with me ten years ago, he told me with characteristic irony about overcoming in himself the ivory tower syndrome of the researcher and then, more seriously, about the vocation to preach the Word of God today to flesh-and-blood people.

With this openness to all people, Fr. Alexander followed in the steps of the apostle Paul, who instructed his followers with these words: "I urge you, then, be imitators of me" (1 Corinthians 4:16). Like the apostle Paul, Fr. Alexander spoke of eternity in the language of his own time—and for that reason he could have applied to himself the words of the apostle to the gentiles: "I have become all things to all men, that I might by all means save some" (1 Corinthians 9:22). For him, to live was Christ and, united with Christ, to die became gain (Philippians 1:21).

Since Christ is always Golgotha—and Resurrection.

Igumen Ignatiy (Krekshin)

(translated by Fr. Maxym Lysack)

On the Road to Church

CHAPTER 1

1

THE GARDEN GATE

On this particular Sunday, September 9, 1990, as he did every Sunday, Fr. Alexander Men got up very early in the morning to celebrate the liturgy in the little country church some twenty-five miles away, a church he had been serving for the past twenty years. Carrying his ever-present briefcase, he pushed open the garden gate and walked rapidly toward the station to take a suburban train coming from Moscow. In the morning mist, he took the narrow path through some trees which were beginning to lose their leaves. A long day lay ahead of him. He would certainly be busy until the beginning of the afternoon when, without losing any time, he would have to take another train back to Moscow. There in the Volkhonka Street cultural center, he would give the second half of a lecture on Christianity.

In 1988, the Soviet authorities had changed their policy toward believers. From that time on, Fr. Alexander openly pursued the activities which, up to that time, he had carried on in near secrecy: he worked to transmit the Gospel to his fellow citizens. On September 1, 1990, he had just celebrated the thirtieth anniversary of his ordination. Ever since the change in policy, he had not had a single moment's rest. His situation was unique in the Soviet Union: for seventy years, believers had been reduced to silence, and Fr. Alexander, who had been under the eye of a whole team of KGB agents, was now continually invited to speak in schools, institutes, clubs, and cultural centers. At Easter he had baptized sixty adults. He spent his energies without thinking twice, while his friends and family worried about him. Fr. Alexander, though, paid no attention to their advice. He certainly had appeared anxious at recent times, though, and this was very much out of character for him. He indeed loved nature, and the few minutes spent walking the length of the wood as the autumn colors danced on the first rays of the sun, no doubt strengthened him. The landscape in that area did not seem to have any particular character, and yet the place was special. The Holy Trinity-St. Sergius[5] Monastery, an important center for the Russian Orthodox Church, was located a few miles from there. There, in the beginning of the fourteenth century, St. Sergius had founded a hermitage in the middle of the forest, which gave Russia a great spiritual inspiration after having been deeply wounded by the invasion of the terrible Mongol warriors of Genghis Khan. Andrei Rublev had been a monk there, and it was for this monastery that he had painted the famous icon of the Holy Trinity. St. Sergius was born in a nearby village and had often taken the very path on which Fr. Alexander was walking...

Some time later, his wife, who had stayed home, opened the window and heard a groaning sound. She ran into the garden and, behind the gate, she saw a man on the ground in a pool of blood. Running into the house, she called an ambulance and the police. When she went out again, the ambulance had already arrived. "Why don't you do something?" she asked the doctors. "It's too late," they answered. She finally moved toward the man; there was a lot of blood, but she did not dare look. Then she asked: "Has my husband arrived?" Someone asked if he had been wearing a gray hat. They had found such a hat with a big hole in it.

Somewhat later, witnesses came forward who had passed Fr. Alexander going in the other direction: bleeding profusely, he had turned around and walked to his house. He had not wanted anyone to help him. He must have collapsed in front of the gate, having lost nearly all his blood from a deep gash in the back of his head, caused by an axe. The circumstances of the crime and the precision of the blow seem to indicate that the attack was carefully prepared and carried out by professionals.

But why did they choose such a weapon?

"We have only just begun to free ourselves from fear," wrote a journalist the day after the murder. "The axe is an excellent way to bring to their senses those who have tasted liberty, to sober them up, and to refresh their memory."[6]

Russian peasants used axes to pursue foreign invaders, the enemy. The axe was the traditional symbol of popular justice, of the punishment of traitors.

The axe was also used to threaten Jews during the pogroms, and Fr. Alexander was of Jewish origin. Are we not in fact dealing with an anti-Semitic crime?

Indeed, after his death, certain periodicals, which for one or two years were the voice of the most extreme Russian nationalism, violently attacked Fr. Alexander while claiming that his murder had been a plot of "anti-Russian and anti-Orthodox forces that he had served all his life," and which may have decided to use him one last time to stir up hatred between Jews and Russians. "May his death be a lesson to all those in the Church who flirt with Satanic forces."[7]

Fr. Alexander himself was worried by the recent rise of xenophobia in which he saw the seeds of a Russian fascism.

Even in the ranks of the most conservative element of the clergy, Fr. Alexander was not at all appreciated. This was especially true among the monks, notably those of the Trinity-St. Sergius Monastery whose blue and gold cupolas are visible from the back of his garden. Is it possible, however, to go so far as to suspect the monks of having inspired the murder? Some indeed have made such accusations.

Should we not rather place this crime with the murders of other priests savagely killed by the secret services of various Eastern European countries, Fr. Popieluszko, for example, who was drowned by agents of the Polish police in 1984? At the very moment Fr. Alexander was killed, rumors of troop movements were heard in Moscow, and the preparations for the putsch of August 1991 were beginning to be put in place.

We know very well that the members of the former communist bureaucracy often exploited any form of aggressive chauvinism in order to preserve or restore their power; indeed, the first ultra-nationalist Russian groups which appeared around 1987-88 were mostly manipulated by the KGB. It is quite possible, therefore, that the Soviet secret police played this card. The speed an energy of the inquiry in denying any kind of political crime is very suspicious, especially in light of the fact that the police found no trace of the killer or killers.

Two years later, as expected, the inquiry had found nothing. Will we ever know? We can at least be fairly certain that Fr. Alexander was not killed accidentally, and that his death was directly caused by the force of his public witness and his extraordinary personality.

The Soviet press widely covered Fr. Alexander's death. Within three days after his death, Izvestia paid tribute to his memory; as a result, the author of the article received telephone death threats. A woman called to insult him: "Well, well! What do we have here? Why didn't his God help him?"[8] Was this woman even aware that these were words spoken by passers-by some two thousand years ago at the foot of the cross: "He trusted in God; let God deliver him now, if He desires him..."[9]

The idea of death was quite familiar to Fr. Alexander. He often reminded people that we are only sojourners in this world: "We have come from mystery, and we return to mystery." We should not be fearful, but instead become very aware of the value of life. "The thought that someday we will be taken ought to stimulate us; it should keep us from letting ourselves go, from slacking off, from sinking into inaction and meaninglessness."[10]

Ever since it had become possible for him to work openly, Fr. Alexander seemed to be in a hurry, as if time were running out for him. Did he think that the new political situation would not last, and that he had to make the most of passing circumstances? "If I do not do today what I have to do," he once said, "I will regret having let the time pass by."[11]

Many of his friends think that he had a premonition of his death. More and more frequently, he returned to the theme of life's fragility. "We are always on the edge of death...You know yourselves how little it takes to cut the lifeline of a man."[12]

On the Sunday before his death, Fr. Alexander started a Sunday school in his parish for the village children. What an event: a completely legal religious course in the Soviet Union. We can imagine his joy; he had dreamt of this for a long time. However, on that truly festive day, to the surprise of all, he began his presentation in this way: "My dear children, you know that one day you will all die..."

FR. ALEXANDER'S FUNERAL
METROPOLITAN JUVENALY (CENTER), VLADIMIR ARKIPOV (RIGHT) THE PRESENT PASTOR
OF THE CHURCH OF NOVAYA DERVNIA

FR. ALEXANDER'S FUNERAL
FR. ALEXANDER BORISOV, AND, BEHIND HIM, FR. VLADIMIR LAPSHIN, BOTH PRIESTS OF THE DOWNTOWN
MOSCOW PARISH OF STS. COSMOS AND DAMIAN

One of his friends, a woman, had tried to persuade him to slow the rhythm of his activities:

> "You're not taking care of yourself at all. You're not a child anymore. You don't belong just to yourself..."
> "I must hurry," he answered. "I have very little time left. I must still accomplish something."
> "Is there something wrong with your heart?" she asked.
> "No, it's not a health problem; everything's OK there but that's the way things are. Believe me, I know."

Another day, when he was trying to get a taxi, the person he was with complained and sighed about the length of the wait. Fr. Alexander answered, "I don't need a taxi but a hearse."[13]

Did he really have a mystical premonition or did he simply feel that he was in danger? He had no doubt received threatening letters, but he had regularly received such threats for many years. Maybe the latest ones were more explicit? Had he perhaps been warned by other, more explicit, signs?

Fr. Alexander's death caused a great stir. Only after this tragedy did the whole country discover him, begin to appreciate his importance, even at the hightest political levels. The president of the USSR, Mikhail Gorbachev, expressed "deep regrets." Boris Yeltsin asked the Supreme Soviet of Russia, that is, the parliament, of which he was President at the time, to observe a minute of silence, and sent a wreath for Fr. Alexander's tomb.

In Europe, Cardinal Lustiger, the archbishop of Paris, who had spoken to Fr. Alexander during a trip to the USSR, expressed his sadness:

"I am grieved by the murder of Fr. Men, whom I met in his parish near Moscow in May, 1989. He had a great spiritual and intellectual influence. He was a man of peace. I was able to meet several adults baptized by him. This savage killing is a tragedy for the whole USSR which, more than ever in its history, needs the Gospel message. By killing him who has given his life for his brothers, Fr. Alexander's murderer not only opposed God, but also attacked his own nation. I pray for Fr. Men, for his family and friends, for his parish, and for the whole Orthodox Church which has been so painfully wounded."

The Patriarch of Moscow underlined the mystery of this death in a message he wrote, to be read on the day of Fr. Alexander's funeral:

"From a strictly human point of view, it seems that only today, finally, has the time come when Fr. Alexander's talent for preaching the Word of God and organizing an authentic parish community can be seen in all its fullness."

The policy of cultural liberation coming from perestroika began with the authorization of a film called Repentance. At the end of the movie, there is an old lady who asks about the road that leads to the church. This image has remained ever since in people's minds as a symbol of a country rediscovering the meaning of true values after seventy years of ideological wandering, of a country coming back to faith. Fr. Alexander was killed while on his way to celebrate the liturgy, precisely on the road leading to the church...

His funeral was celebrated on the day the Orthodox Church commemorates the beheading of St. John the Baptist, called the Forerunner because he came to prepare the way...

One day in 1984, when he was in great danger from the KGB, Fr. Alexander confided the following to his friends: "I have told myself, in my inner heart, that I have accomplished my mission, that I have done what I could for the Church of Christ and that I am ready to stand before the Lord."[14]

Some days before his death, Fr. Alexander had concluded a lecture about a Russian Orthodox nun, an emigre from Paris, who had been part of the resistance during the war and who had been killed by the Nazis: "To give one's self completely is to fulfill the Gospel. Only in this way can the world be saved."[15] To give one's self completely...

The Descent into the Catacombs

CHAPTER 2

J. STALIN IN 1935

SOLOVKI: THE CAPTIVE CHURCH

Fr. Alexander Men was born on January 22, 1935.[16] Soviet power at that time was loudly boasting of its triumph. The Communist Party congress of the previous year had been named the "Congress of the Victors." The objectives of the first industrialization plan had been reached in four, instead of five, years. The collectivization of the farms had been achieved, but at the cost of millions of peasants deported, killed, or starved. The whole society had been brought into line.

Under the guidance of the Communist Party and its glorious leader, Joseph Stalin, the Soviet people were accomplishing heroic exploits: soldiers were ceaselessly guarding the borders; the NKVD (the forerunner of the KGB) was destroying the enemies of the people; pilots were flying higher, farther, and faster; the Stakanovists were breaking productivity records; and musicians were winning international competitions... This was the line everyone was hearing on the radio and reading in the papers.

The previous month, the party chief in Leningrad had been assassinated, most likely on the Kremlin's orders. Stalin used the occasion to launch the "Great Terror," and the secret police undertook massive arrests. Soon after, the Moscow trials opened, during which the accused admitted to the most unbelievable crimes. They confessed, for example, to having put ground glass into the country's butter production. The gulag, whose "citizens" were counted in the millions, never ceased to grow.

Nonetheless, a large section of the population, especially the youth, was convinced that they were participating in the birth of a new society, one that would fulfill all the hopes of mankind. And what is more, how many intellectuals throughout the world saw the USSR as "a land where utopia was becoming a reality"?[17] People justified the violence by saying that a world was being built where there would be no more violence. "You can't make an omelet without breaking some eggs," people said. The very words pity and charity seemed to be outdated. Everything was subordinated to political efficacy. People believed that, just by obeying science, they could build paradise on earth. Atheism dominated everyone's thinking; nearly everyone thought that only old, uneducated women could believe in God. The State used all its weight to keep "retrograde parents from poisoning the minds of their children with religious nonsense."

The League of Militant Atheists quickly boasted of thirty million members; it published countless papers, magazines, books, and brochures in addition to operating dozens of antireligious museums. During a visit to one of these museums in 1936, Andre Gide was surprised to discover the following inscription over an image of Christ: "A legendary person who never existed."[18] Even though no one could suspect Gide of being sympathetic to the Church, he said that he would be surprised if the Gospel could ever be entirely eliminated from the USSR.

All the institutions of the Orthodox Church, as well as those of other religious bodies, were almost entirely destroyed. More than ninety-five percent of Orthodox churches had been closed. Only a few bishops were still tolerated. No monastery, no seminary existed anywhere. How many bishops, priests, monks, and nuns had been tortured, massacred, shot; how many died of exhaustion in the terrible Solovki camp? How many were arrested, released, then condemned and sent to a camp; how many, after having finished their sentence, were condemned again to a new prison term when they should have been freed? How many found themselves somewhere in the gulag, building the White Sea canal? Will we ever know how many lay people were imprisoned because of their religious beliefs? How many were killed? How many died during the "Great Terror"? Never since the time of the Roman emperor Diocletian had the Christian world undergone such a terrible persecution.

In the period preceding the Revolution, the moral authority of the Orthodox Church had been seriously undermined by its submission to the tsarist government. Peter the Great, two centuries before, had eliminated the patriarchate, which had governed the Church up to that time. Ever since Peter's time, the tsars had claimed to be the protectors of the Church, but in fact, they reduced it to become just another department of the government. During the reign of Nicholas II, this dependence became spectacularly obvious for everyone to see when the bishops themselves fell into the hands of Rasputin, the "guru" of the imperial family.

The profound evolution of Russian society in the eighteenth and nineteenth centuries left the Church completely by the wayside. The intelligentsia had entirely turned away from it. Nonetheless, Orthodox missionaries were carrying the Gospel, translated into dozens of Siberian languages, even to the Pacific Ocean and beyond. In addition, a spiritual revival was beginning under the inspiration of prayer-filled men, of whom the most famous was Saint Seraphim of Sarov (1759-1833). In the middle of the nineteenth century, an obscure monastery at Optina, about two hundred miles southwest of Moscow, suddenly became a center to which crowds of faithful flocked. In the monasteries, experienced monks had always helped the younger monks advance in their spiritual life, but what was new at Optina was that the monks, called startsy or elders, began to help lay people who came to talk to them.[19] The monks guided the people, helping them come to God. They became "spiritual fathers", while the faithful who followed their direction became their "spiritual children". The fathers received people from morning to night, listening, consoling, counseling, teaching. They were open to everyone, rich or poor, noble or peasant. They carried on their ministry often despite the hesitation of some in the Church hierarchy; some bishops felt that all this activity just created disorder. Through Optina, a bridge between the Church and culture was re-established, and many great figures of the time visited the startsy. In his novel The Brothers Karamazov, Dostoevsky evoked at length the atmosphere that reigned at Optina. After a conversation with one of the startsy, Tolstoy exclaimed, "I only chatted with him and already my soul feels greatly lightened."[20]

At the end of the nineteenth century, a parish priest attained great popularity in all levels of society, but especially among the lower classes. He was Father John, the priest of Kronstadt, the island and military port across from Saint Petersburg. Kronstadt became the home of many outcasts from the capital: the jobless, the poverty-stricken, and the homeless. Father John provided them with workshops, a hospice, a hospital, a soup kitchen, and other things. His fame spread all over the country, and he was invited to visit every corner of Russia. He celebrated the liturgy, preached, heard confessions, and healed many sick people by his prayers. However, the veneration of which he was the object gave birth to a fanatical sect, and he sanctioned the Union of the Russian People, a party of ultra-nationalists formed in 1905. (Some present-day movements find their inspiration in this party, especially in its virulent anti-Semitism.)

At the beginning of the twentieth century, the impenetrable wall between the intelligentsia and religion broke down. A whole

PATRIARCH TIKHON

BISHOP SERGIUS

THE COUNCIL OF 1917 - 1918

St. Seraphim of Sarov

St. John of Kronstadt

series of lay authors developed an original religious philosophy that struck a chord in a wide segment of the population. Even certain members of the clergy began to take an interest in it. Pavel Florensky, according to his friends the Russian Leonardo da Vinci, was one of the most brilliant members of this generation. He was named professor of theology at the Moscow Theological Academy, located inside the walls of the Holy Trinity-Saint Sergius Monastery, and was finally ordained a priest. He finished his days in the gulag. Most of the other authors were expelled from the USSR and pursued their work abroad.

In 1905, the first wave of revolutionary fervor swept over the country. The tsar had to make concessions on all fronts. The Church also got caught up in the excitement; various associations were created, petitions were circulated, and priests began to complain about the bishops' power. As for the bishops themselves, they were less and less willing to bend to the heavy weight of the state's protection and began hoping to restore the patriarchate. There was a growing acceptance of the idea that the Church needed an aggiornamento. The tsar agreed that a council should be called to regulate all these questions. This local council of the Russian Orthodox Church was carefully prepared, but could not be convoked until after the fall of Nicholas II. In the scope and extent of its proposed reforms, the council could be compared to Vatican II. The council finally opened to great pomp and circumstance in Moscow on August 15, 1917. Several weeks later, fierce battles were raging in the Kremlin as a result of the Bolsheviks' taking power in Petrograd, no longer Saint Petersburg but not yet Leningrad. At this time the council voted to restore the patriarchate. Metropolitan Tikhon[21] was chosen as the new patriarch, a man known and liked for his simplicity, humility, and goodness. The council also voted on a whole series of important decisions concerning, especially, the re-organization of parish structures. It was forced to adjourn, however, before being able to finish its reform program.

The new political power and the Church immediately came into conflict. In the eyes of the Bolsheviks, the Church was compromised politically by its close ties to the former regime. In addition, the Bolshevik ideology denounced all religion as a psychological disorder. Marx had taught that "the suppression of religion as people's illusory happiness is necessary for their real happiness."[22] Lenin thought that the very idea of God was intolerable. He wrote, "Any flirtation with God is the most unspeakable depravity. Any defense, any justification of the idea of God, even the most subtle, even the most refined, warrants whatever reaction it provokes."[23] Moreover, even if the Orthodox Church was the first target of government attacks, no other religious organization was spared in the end. The setting up of Bolshevik political power brought violence all across the country. In the name of nationalizing the property and goods of the Church, acts of aggression against churches and monasteries multiplied. The patriarch reacted by inviting all the faithful to remain firm in the faith, and by excommunicating all those, wherever they might be, who "sow the seeds of evil, hatred, and fratricidal struggle." On January 23, 1918, the Bolshevik authorities passed a decree separating the Church from the State, a law that also included a separation of schools from the Church. The content of the law, however, did not correspond to its title. As believers were to explain with humor later on, the Church was separated from the State, but not the State from the Church. The law attempted to deprive the Church of its means of action, both legal and material. In particular, parish associations were not recognized as legal bodies, and religious education was only authorized on a private basis. Subsequent regulations made clear that religious education could only be given at the request of the parents, in private homes, and to a maximum of three children.

The application of the decree brought with it all sorts of injustices: churches and numerous monasteries were arbitrarily closed, priests were arrested in the middle of services, others were forced to sweep the streets, and priestly vestments were made into revolutionary flags. In less than a year, twenty bishops, dozens of priests, deacons, monks , and nuns were killed. In order to fight against popular piety, antireligious plays were put on. The reliquaries of venerated saints were opened. A Communist handbook of the time affirmed, "Showing the people 'incorruptible' relics is an effective means...There is nothing better for exposing to the gullible masses the gross deceit on which all religion in general rests--and especially the Russian Orthodox religion."[24]

The relics of Saint Sergius were profaned. The monastery he founded was closed and turned into an antireligious museum. The little town that had grown up around the monastery was named Zagorsk after a revolutionary. Today it has taken back its former name: Sergeev Posad.

The civil war between the Red and White armies gave rise to an orgy of violence as the White forces tried to regain power from the Bolsheviks. Communications became impossible between certain parts of the Church administration. The Patriarch authorized the bishops of isolated dioceses, cut off from Moscow, to make decisions without reference to the central government. Even though the Patriarch avoided taking sides in the political struggle, he had to face a new assault on the Church after the final victory of the Bolsheviks. A terrible famine fell on the country, and in 1922 the authorities ordered the seizure and sale of all valuable objects in the churches, for the relief of the famine victims. The Patriarch himself had taken the initiative in this matter, but had opposed the seizure of consecrated objects such as liturgical vessels. Nonetheless, the government forged ahead with its plan, and confiscated even the consecrated objects. In many places the faithful tried to prevent such acts. Violent incidents resulted, and the government used them as a pretext to arrest, to try, and to execute many among the clergy. A secret letter from Lenin, however, has shown that the provocation was deliberately premeditated so as to allow "the execution of the greatest possible number" of clergy.[25] Patriarch Tikhon, called as a witness for one of these trials, was himself indicted and put under arrest.

During this time, many groups of priests, called renovators, were organized. They wanted to see new reforms put into effect, for example, the modernization of the liturgy. Such changes could have been implemented by the 1917-1918 council if its work had not been interrupted. Other reforms were simply not acceptable in the Orthodox tradition, such as married bishops.[26] In the contemporary Orthodox Church, parish priests are generally married and have families; bishops, on the other hand, are always chosen from among the monks, and are therefore necessarily celibate. The renovators said they were in favor of a more social orientation of the Church, and espoused a collaboration with the Bolsheviks. These priests took advantage of a confused situation and, with the support of the authorities, carried out a veritable putsch. They formed a college that was supposed to govern the Church; convoked a council that deposed the Patriarch; and attempted to rally the bishops and parishes; not however, without the help of the NKVD, who arrested their adversaries. By this collusion, the renovators compromised the very idea of liturgical reform for quite some time. Reform and collaboration were associated in the minds of the faithful.

Under the pressure of international opinion, the Soviet government freed Patriarch Tikhon, but only after he had expressed regrets for his "anti-Soviet activities." He then actively worked to restore unity to the Orthodox Church, and the majority of those bishops and priests who had gone over to the renovators began to recognize his authority once again. In addition, he made many declarations to the effect that the Church, being neither Red nor White, recognized and supported the Soviet power. The Patriarch died in 1925, leaving a will in which he indicated the names of three bishops who were called upon to replace him, one after the other, until a council could be called to elect a new Patriarch. The first two bishops were already in exile, and the third was soon arrested. The last bishop designated his successor, Metropolitan Sergius[27], who was also promptly arrested. The metropolitan was released after several months, and with several bishops published a declaration of loyalty to the Bolshevik authorities, a statement that aroused much discussion among the clergy. Patriarch Tikhon had no doubt already begun normalizing the relations of the Church with the Soviet government, but tried to remain somewhat more neutral. In his declaration of allegiance, Metropolitan Sergius used a formula that has since become legendary: "We want to be Orthodox and at the same time to recognize the Soviet Union as our civil motherland. Her joys and successes are our joys and successes, her setbacks our setbacks." He thanked the Soviet authorities for "the interest they show for all the religious needs of the Orthodox population." Nevertheless, many argued that the metropolitan had no right to bind the whole Church, since he was only, to put it simply, the replacement of a replacement temporarily hindered from doing his job. Many also reproached the metropolitan for abusively shunting aside the bishops who did not bow to his wishes and who especially did not approve of his relying on the civil powers to eliminate opposition, as the renovators had done. Several bishops broke communion with Metropolitan Sergius, considering that they had to administer their dioceses provisionally under the same conditions that had prevailed during the civil war when outlying areas were cut off from the patriarchate. They thus gave birth to a whole underground movement.

A BUILDING OF THE OPTINA MONASTERY IN 1980

A new phase in the antireligious struggle opened at the very moment when the collectivization process was launched. The signal was given by the publication in 1929 of a declaration determining the status of religious associations. This text, which was not abolished officially until 1990, essentially recapitulated all the antireligious legislation of the preceding years. Bishops and priests were again arrested in great numbers. The closing of churches picked up, and many of them were demolished. Icons and religious books were burned by the car load. Work was reorganized according to a new calendar which divided the week into five - and then six-days, eliminating Sunday as a day of rest.

In 1935, the Church seemed to have been eliminated from society; it had practically no visible existence. Religious life had not been destroyed, however; it continued, mostly in secret, in the catacombs -the catacombs of the twentieth century.

THE TRINITY-SAINT-SERGIUS MONESTERY

In the Shadow of
St. Sergius

CHAPTER 3

ALEXANDER AND HIS MOTHER

VERA (LEFT) AND HELENA

Alexander Men's parents belonged to a genera-
tion that, on the whole, had few doubts or uncertainties, and
busied themselves constructing the future society without asking
metaphysical questions. After studies in the technical institute
in Kiev, Alexander's father received a diploma in textile engi-
neering and threw himself completely into his work. Although
of Jewish origin, he lost his faith in his childhood through the
influence of one of his teachers, without at the same time becoming a militant atheist. Any kind of religious idea was totally
foreign to him, but he was tolerant.

In contrast, Alexander's mother Elena[28] had a very deep religious
consciousness. She was also born of Jewish parents and was raised
by her mother to love God as Creator of the universe and Lover
of all men. "When I first heard about the fear of God," she
remembered, "I asked my mother, 'We love God, so how can we
fear Him?' Mother answered me, 'We should fear causing Him
pain by doing something bad.' I was completely satisfied with
that answer."

Elena had also been very much under the influence of her grandmother, that is, Alexander's great-grandmother. The family
proudly told how she had been healed by John of Kronstadt himself. At Kharkov in 1890, widowed and with seven children, she
became ill. The doctors could do nothing for her. One day, a

neighbor told her that the famous preacher was passing through town and persuaded her to go see him. The church and the town square were filled with people, but the neighbor helped Alexander's great-grandmother make a path through the crowd to Fr. John. He looked at her and said, "I know that you are Jewish, but I see in you a deep faith in God. Pray to the Lord and He will heal you." A month later, she was completely restored to health.

Even from childhood, Elena was attracted to Christianity. When she was nine years old, she told her mother that she wanted to be baptized. The announcement was like a bombshell, and her brother had to break a window in order to divert their mother's anger. Some years later, she began going to services in a Baptist community. One day, she attended a ceremony during which adults were baptized in a river; she was very impressed. Such contacts with the Baptists again provoked disputes in the household. After Elena and her family were finally reconciled, her cousin Vera[29] came to Kharkov and took her to Moscow[30], where she settled permanently and got married.

Vera was older than Elena by several years; she was a very sensitive, unsettled woman who, like Elena, was constantly searching. Later on in life, Vera told how, at the age of eighteen, she felt an inexplicable sadness every Sunday. One morning, while she was working in a sort of summer camp, she went out into the country and heard a far-off bell ringing. "For everyone it is Sunday, but not for you," one of the children told her[31]. Ten or so years before the arrival of her cousin Elena in Moscow, Vera became friends with a young girl her age who belonged to one of the most active circles of Orthodox Christians in Moscow.

One of the purposes of the 1917-1918 council was to restore the parishes to the status of "little Churches" on the model of the first Christian communities. Patriarch Tikhon was himself very partial to the renewal of community life in the parishes. In line with this objective, after the Revolution ordinary Christians began to form small groups around certain priests with strong personalities; these groups could almost be called base communities before the invention of the term.

At that time, there were two especially active communities in Moscow, very closely related. The better known of the two was centered in the church of Saint Nicholas on Maroseika Street[32], served at first by Fr. Alexei Mechev and then, after his death, by his son Fr. Sergei Mechev. A lay fraternity had been formed around this church in October 1917. The second group was in the parish of Ss. Kyrios and John[33], where Fr. Seraphim was the priest.[34]

Despite an early call to priesthood, Fr. Seraphim had studied to become a technician and worked a secular trade before being ordained a priest in 1919, at thirty-nine years of age. Having chosen to remain unmarried, he could have become a monk sometime later, but Patriarch Tikhon himself asked him to take the parish of Ss. Kyrios and John. Before the Revolution, Fr. Seraphim often visited the Optina monastery, being under the spiritual direction of one of the startsy. He shared the spirit of Optina, which he manifested in guiding his parishioners: he was always available to them, paid each one individual attention, and was always concerned about their problems.

Fr. Seraphim never accepted the 1927 declaration and went underground, attaching himself to Bishop Afanassy[35], one of the bishops who had refused to recognize the authority of Metropolitan Sergius. Fr. Seraphim's link with Bishop Afanassy was nearly exclusively spiritual, since after the Revolution the bishop's life was nothing but a long series of arrests and deportations to

THE CHURCH ON MAROSEIKA St

FR. SERGEI METCHEV

FR. ALEXEI MECHEV

BISHOP ASANASSY

FR. SERAPHIM BATIUKOV

the gulag. Only rarely could anyone actually meet him. After having to change his hide-out many times, Fr. Seraphim finally found refuge in a house in Zagorsk; two nuns lived there after having been expelled from their convent. A small chapel was set up in one of the rooms, where he celebrated the liturgy in secret.

From this house, he continued to support his spiritual children as well as the former parishioners from St. Nicholas parish, who came to him after Sergei Mechev had been arrested. Obviously they could not come visit him except by taking all kinds of precautions, as though they were conspirators.

Vera's friend was one of the spiritual children of Fr. Seraphim, and made it possible for Vera to write him letters. Depite her love for Jesus Christ, Vera was reluctant to ask to be baptized. She was held back by the traditional prejudices of the intelligentsia against the Orthodox Church. There was also the atmosphere of conspiracy, the impossibility of opening herself to the people around her. She had to invent a lie just to be able to go see Fr. Seraphim in Zagorsk. In addition, if Jews wanted to be baptized, people often used to accuse them of opportunism. Vera was also tortured by the fear that her baptism might be interpreted as an act of betrayal, even though Christians were persecuted at that time. Any adult who received baptism, especially if he worked in the educational system, exposed himself to very serious risks.[36]

Elena's character was less tormented than her cousin's. The birth of her son Alexander made it possible for her to come to a rapid decision. On September 3, 1935, Vera's friend accompanied Elena and the little Alik on the train to Zagorsk and led them to Fr. Seraphim's house where the priest was waiting. There in the little house, he baptized both the mother and the son. Vera also finally decided to be baptized. Elena had a second son Pavel, and Vera naturally was chosen godmother. Vera never married, but became very attached to Elena's two children, and helped her raise them. Fr. Seraphim came to love the two cousins very deeply, telling them one day that they were closer to him than his own sisters. One day when some visitors asked him about the two little boys, Fr. Seraphim answered, "They are mine!"

Elena and Vera regularly made the trip from Moscow to Zagorsk to visit Fr. Seraphim. With some of Fr. Seraphim's other spiritual children, the two women participated in the services he celebrated as often as they could.

Vera once related the story of her first Easter night liturgy: "Before beginning the service, the priest sent someone out into the street to make sure that the singing could not be heard. Then the paschal vigil began, and the little house was transformed into a temple of light. Everyone was united by the same, incomparable feeling: the joy of the Resurrection. The procession was held inside the izba[37], in the vestibule and the hallway. The priest gave everyone an icon so that all could participate.[38]" Is not this the way the first Christians held their services during the time of the Romanpersecutions? The "Catacombs of the Twentieth Century" is precisely the name that Vera gave to her memoirs.[39]

In January 1941, Elena's husband was arrested, not however for a political reason, but on a charge of malpractice. At the end of the year he was acquitted and released, but during the time he was in jail the family's financial situation was very difficult.

On Sunday, June 22, 1941, Vera went to Zagorsk alone. The day was to be most beautiful; the wather was magnificent. On that day the Church celebrated the feast of All Saints of Russia. When she opened the door, Alik said to her, "Please ask grandfather (that was his name for Fr. Seraphim): will there still be war when I am big?" The preceding night, Hitler's army had crossed the Soviet border, and the country was once again to endure terrible suffering. Stalin was holed up for ten days unable to act. Metropolitan Sergius, however, wrote a pastoral letter on the very day of the invasion, calling on all Orthodox to defend the country. When Stalin did reappear, he greeted everyone with the usual "Comrades and Citizens" but then added the greeting usually used by priests at the beginning of their sermons: "Brothers and Sisters!" A curious change in vocabulary!

Through Vera, Fr. Seraphim advised Elena immediately to find a place to live in Zagorsk or in the surrounding area and to move there with the children. Her friends and acquaintances were very surprised since, with the Germans approaching at the time, Muscovites were trying to get out of the capital. Fr. Seraphim was convinced, however, that Zagorsk was under the protection of St. Sergius.

Fr. Seraphim died at the beginning of 1942. He was buried secretly in the basement. Some time before, sensing that death was near, he insisted on hearing Alik's first confession even though the child was only seven years old. "With grandfather, I felt like I was in heaven with God," Alik said. "He spoke to me so simply, as though we were just chatting."

As for Fr. Seraphim, he often made a prediction to the two cousins: "Thanks to what you are enduring and to the serious way you are raising him, your Alik will someday be a great man." Late on, Fr. Alexander was to express his eternal gratitude to his mother and her cousin for having maintained the flame of faith and exposed him to the Gospel in such difficult times. Those were times when the faith was persecuted and seemed on the road to extinction, times when famous Christians did not resist but denied the faith." It was a tragic period which required a lot of courage and faithfulness."[40]

Before his death, Fr. Seraphim put his spiritual children into the hands of two men who were very close to him, Fr. Ieraks[41] and Fr. Piotr Shipkov.[42] Fr. Ieraks was also an underground priest living near Zagorsk. Fr. Piotr had been ordained by Patriarch Tikhon, and had even been his secretary for a while. After many years in the gulag, he was hired as an accountant in a Zagorsk factory. However, after being denounced, the two priests were arrested in 1943, along with the nun[43] who had remained in Fr. Seraphim's house. At the same time, after having spent many years in a camp and having undergone exile in Siberia, Bishop Afanassy was also arrested. All were condemned for being heads of an "underground religious organization." The police even went so far as to dig up Fr. Seraphim's body. "I will strike the shepherd, and the sheep of the flock will be scattered."[44]

Nonetheless, there was still one izba in Zagorsk[45] where a small underground community of nuns met. Fr. Seraphim had been their spiritual father until his death. After his death, the higumena, Mother Maria, continued to encourage the young Alexander and to help him in his spiritual development. In a letter, Fr. Alexander indicated the impact that these men and women of God had made on him:

"Fr. Seraphim was a disciple of the startsy of Optina and a friend of Fr. Alexei Mechev. He baptized my mother and me, and for many years undertook the spiritual direction of our whole family. After his death, his successors took charge; they were people of great spiritual power, with the wisdom and illumination of the startsy. My childhood and my teenage years were spent near them and under the shadow of St. Sergius. I lived there with my mother, who is now dead,

FR. PIOTR SKIPKOV

MOTHER MARIA

FR. IERAKS

FR. SERAPHIM'S IZBA IN ZAGORSK

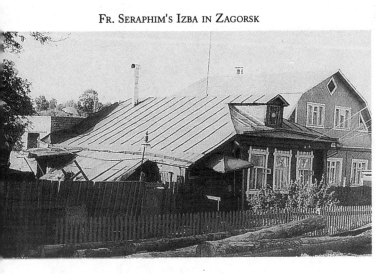

and she had a great deal to do with determining my spiritual life and orientation. She lived an ascetic and prayerful life, completely free of hypocrisy, bigotry, and narrowness: traits often present in people in her state. She was always filled with paschal joy, a deep dedication to the will of God, and a feeling of closeness to the spiritual world, in a certain way, like St. Seraphim or St. Francis of Assisi. ... She had a trait similar to the character of the startsy of Optina, a trait so dear to them: openness to people, to their problems, and to their searching; openness to the world. It is precisely this quality that drew the best representatives of Russian culture to Optina. After a long rupture, Optina did in fact renew the dialogue between the Church and society. It was an undertaking of great, exceptional importance, despite the lack of confidence and opposition of the authorities. In Fr. Seraphim and Mother Maria, I saw a living extension of that dialogue. This idea of dialogue with the world has stuck with me all my life; it should never be interrupted. I have always felt I should participate in that conversation with whatever meager force I have.[46"]

The Formative Years

CHAPTER 4

THE 1945 COUNCIL

A MONK DRAWN BY ALEXANDER
AS A TEENAGER

For a while, people thought that the trials and tribulations of the war might have changed the political system, but nothing of the kind happened. Things did noticeably change for the Orthodox Church, however, because Stalin was led to revise his policy in relation to religion. In order to mobilize the population against the aggressor at the begining of hostilities, the Soviet authorities appealed to the people's national sentiment rather than to a defence of the communist ideal. Russian identity is closely tied to Orthodoxy. What is more, events showed the rulers that religion had not been eliminated with the building of socialism as all their handbooks had prophesied. In those territories invaded by Nazi troops, the inhabitants had spontaneously reopened the churches which, from then on, were never empty. The German authorities made no attempt to interfere. Finally, in order to improve relations with its new allies the United States and Great Britain, the USSR needed to change its image for the better by reassuring the outside world about the situation of believers.

In September 1943, Stalin received Metropolitan Sergius and two other bishops, and authorized a synod of bishops which elected Metropolitan Sergius Patriarch. The new Patriarch did not live long, and a new council, called in February 1945, several months before the end of the war, elected Alexis I[47] as the new patriarch. The Orthodox Church was able to rebuild its internal administration by naming a bishop at the head of each diocese. Even though the council was very short with no debates, it had time to adopt a new Church law which, most importantly, confirmed that priests were the heads of their parishes. In reality, according to the civil law of 1929, all parishes had to be constituted as an association of at least twenty members[48] and governed by an executive administration of three persons. The priest seemed to be excluded from this structure. Now the 1945 Church law provided that each parish be placed under the direction of its pastor, the ex officio president of an executive administration of four, not three, members. This structure, although in line with the permanent tradition of the Church, was in open conflict with the 1929 civil law, but the government seemed not to notice the difference.

With the same blind eye, the authorities neglected to close the churches and monasteries that had been reopened in that part of the country formerly occupied by German troops. In the East and the North, however, which had not been occupied, there were far fewer reopenings. For example, the only monastery allowed to receive new monks was the Trinity-Saint Sergius Monastery.

Of all the schools that had prepared candidates for the priesthood and that had been closed at the Revolution, only the Theological Academy of Moscow and an attached seminary were reopened, first in the buildings of the Novodevichy Monastery and then transferred to the Trinity-Saint Sergius Monastery at Zagorsk. The seminary provided the basic theological education necessary for any priest wanting to work in a parish. After this first stage of preparation, certain students could pursue their studies at the academy. A seminary and academy were also permitted in Leningrad; seminaries were reopened in a few other cities, as well. The Journal of the Moscow Patriarchate, which had been started by Metropolitan Sergius but quickly shut down, started publishing again.

The Church was nonetheless forbidden to have any kind of active prescence in society. It had only the freedom to celebrate religious services. The Church was considered to be somewhat like an Indian reservation: no one would be massacred as long as everyone stayed inside its limits. In the end, what was granted to the Church was the possibility of organizing to satisfy the "religious needs" of the people, according to Marx's ironical expression; needs that were put on the same level as bodily functions. Satisfying such needs was for the Soviet authorities the only reason for liturgical activity.

In addition, the Church remained under strict surveillance. A special agency within the cabinet, the Council for the Affairs of the Orthodox Cchurch, was created to serve as an intermediary between religious organizations and the civil authorities. It also had the task, however, of exercising a permanent control over all the activities of the Church -in close cooperation with the NKVD, of course. The Council's center was in Moscow, but it had a representative in each region. There was a similar council for the other religions, too.

The Soviet political power tried to use the Church for its own ends in foreign affairs. The Orthodox hierarchy was authorized to establish relations with the outside world on the condition that its representatives serve as messengers of Soviet propaganda in circles where communist parties had little influence.

Finally, believers in the camps did not benefit from a general amnesty, any more than did the other interned "citizens" of the gulag. Bishop Afanassy, Fr. Ieraks, and Fr. Piotr continued to serve out their sentences. The arrests of believers continued.

Despite all these problems, the Church was able to get back on its feet. In the immediate post-war period, it benefited from a freedom of action that was somewhat greater than what it would enjoy in subsequent years, when the regime once again cracked down on the Church with all the implacable fury of its ideology. The Church also received new strength from those areas which had been annexed by the USSR after the war, but which had not yet passed under the bulldozer of Sovietization. Priests and bishops exiled form Russia after the Revolution came back. Although their lives were often very difficult, they brought with them a bit of fresh air.

And finally, the Orthodox Church regained its unity. During the war, the renovators had practically lost their last adherents. Those bishops who had broken with Metropolitan Sergius recognized Patriarch Alexei I. If some underground communities still existed, it seems that they were few in number. Thus in 1945, Bishop Afanassy, Fr. Ieraks, and Fr. Piotr managed to get a letter out from their prison camp to their followers. In this letter, they explained their position: the new patriarch had been elected in a canonical manner and incarnated the unity of the Church. If certain acts of Alexei I and the Patriarchate might shock the more fervent Orthodox, the Patriarch himself would have to answer to God, but this was no reason for believers to deprive themselves of the sacraments.[49]

Vera and Elena knew about the letter, but they did not know what to make of it. In the end, Vera decided to go ask the advice of Mother Maria, the higumena of the undergound convent in Zagorsk. When Mother Maria opened the door, Vera asked her, "Well, to which Church do you belong now?" Vera then burst into tears, and the nun comforted her by assuring her of the authenticity of the letter.[50] The time of the catacombs had come to an end; a new time was beginning.

The rebirth of the Church wa especially strong in Moscow. Not only were churches reopened with many people attending the services, but the faithful could also hear talented preachers; in some parishes, they could even attend a whole series of lectures on religious subjects. In one church, a priest put up a screen and illustrated his presentation on the Bible with slides.[51] This renewal of activity lasted about five years, until 1950. Those parishioners who had been active right after the Revolution and who had survived underground or in the gulag tried to reconstitute their circle of friends. The parishioners of the Mechev priests, father and son, attempted to do this. They held meetings in many places but especially at Boris Vassiliev's apartment.[52] As an ethnographer and historian, Vassiliev had written a book on the grat Russian poet Pushkin, but he had also known imprisonment, the camps, and exile. Boris Vassiliev and his wife organized lectures in their home on culture and religion, as well as study groups on the New Testament; his wife also taught a religious course for children.[53] Such initiatives, which had been unthinkable before the war, were not to remain possible for long.

The bonds were very strong between the former spiritual children of the Mechevs, as well as between those of Fr. Seraphim. Vera and Elena were personal friends of the Vassilievs, in whose home Alik was naturally welcome. The young teenager gained a great deal from his contact with the Christian intellectuals he met there. In them, he saw an example of a solid parish community that had been able to preserve its spiritual unity long after the death of its pastors and despite the ups and downs of the time.

Alik was a very gifted and precocious child; he could not get enough learning. When he was ten years old, at the end of the war, Vera explained to him that life cannot be divided into two parts, childhood and adulthood. Life is one, and what is left undone in childhood can never be done later on in life. It is therefore necessary to set serious goals and try to reach them as soon as possible, without losing any time.

Like many other Muscovites at the time, Alik's family had to share one community apartment with several others.[54] There were five people in one single room: two parents, two sons, and cousin Vera. Alexander had to isolate his bed and night table, piled high with books, behind a folding screen. Each night he prepared what he had decided to study the next day and went to bed at 9:00, even if there were interesting guests in the apartment or a good radio program tempted him. He got up early in the morning, and read while everyone else was asleep.[55]

During these early morning study periods, he read works that were rather difficult for his age. He was reading Kant, for example, at thirteen years of age, while his fellow teenagers were learning that Marxist Leninism, naturally enriched by the thoughts of the genius Stalin, was the "only philosophical theory that provided a scientific picture of the world, that defended the principles and scientific methods of explaining nature and society, and that furnished working humanity with the arms necessary for constructing Communism" - and other gibberish.

Alexander had somber memories of the education he received in his school, the School for Boys #554.[56] There were, however, some very strong personalities among his classmates. Some were to attain international reputations later on: such as the poet Voznesensky and the film maker Tarkovsky. One of Alexander's very close friends, Alexander Borisov, was also to become a priest and is today the very active pastor of a parish in the heart of Moscow.

Despite his gifts, Alik was not one of those eggheads at the head of their class, turned in on themselves and incapable of talking to people. On the contrary, his fellow students remembered him as being a friendly type; he participated in school activities with his classmates and was surrounded as much by friends as by books. He wa interested in a great variety of things: literature, poetry, music, and painting. Later on in his life, he took courses in painting and drawing. Some of his paintings and sketches have survived; he also painted icons. He loved to study nature, astronomy, biology and to draw the animals at the zoo. He once wrote the following:

> "From my early childhood, the contemplation of nature has been my 'theologia prima'.[57] I used to go into a forest or a museum of paleontology in the same way I went into a church. And even now, a branch with its leaves or a bird in full flight has for me more meaning than a hundred icons. Even so, pantheism as a religious psychology has always been foreign to me. I always conceived of God as a person, as Someone who is turned in my direction."

It seemed to him that by studying the natural sciences, by observing a slice of something under the microscope for example, he communed with and participated in the divine mystery.[58] He used to say that God had given us two books: the Bible and nature.[59]

Bible reading had awakened his interest in history. He was always searching for the slightest detail that could shed light on biblical events.

Alik thought he would fulfill his mission as a Christian in a scientific or artistic profession.[60] Little by little, however, another vocation was taking shape in him, but he had to have a personal

PATRIARCH ALEXIS

FR. NIKOLAI GOLUBTSOV

ANATOLI VEDERNIKOV

encounter with Christ before this would crystallize. He did have such a personal call at the age of twelve, and decided that he would serve God as a priest.[61] Mother Maria gave him her blessing.[62]

Alexander went to visit the seminary, which was just beginning to get organized. Anatoly Vedernikov, the open and hospitable director of studies, received the young Alexander and told him that as soon as he was of age, he could certainly register as a student.

In the meantime, Alexander did not give up on his general education. He continued to read the great philosophers. Quite by accident, he found the works of some Russian religious thinkers of the early twentieth century who had been exiled on Lenin's orders after the Revolution. These authors, such as Berdyaev and Sergius Bulgakov[63], were completely unknown to Soviet citizens. For a while, Alexander had a passion for Khomiakov[64], a writer with a brilliant mind and of great learning who had been the main inspiration for the Slavophile movement. The objective of this group was to build a new culture on the basis of the Orthodox faith. In the middle of the nineteenth century, Khomiakov had given a great boost to Russian laymen engaged in theological research; this activity was to bear fruit at the very beginning of the twentieth century. This theological orientation soon lost its interest for Alexander because he felt that its judgements on Western Christianity were biased and lacked objectivity.[65] One day when he was about fifteen years old and was visiting a flea market, he discovered a book by Vladimir Soloviev lost among some nails, old shoes, and locks. Soloviev, some would say, had been the real founder of twentieth-century Russian religious thinking.[66] Alexander devoured the book, and later on bought the other books in the series. This author was a revelation for him and he was obviously struck by Soloviev's central idea: a dynamism at the heart of reality unites nature, man, and God Himself in one single process.[67] Soloviev's Christian vision incorporated every aspect of life: the religions and cultures of all peoples and of all periods as well as artistic creation, science, and philosophy. Anything and everything of value was to be brought together and transfigured.[68] The young Alexander also appreciated Soloviev's refusal to idealize former Christian societies and was moved by his action in favor of Christian unity. Alexander took Soloviev as his main intellectual guide without, however, losing his own critical mind. Whole sections of Soloviev's doctrine, such as sophiology and theocracy, had no impact on him. In the same way, Alexander never shared the pessimism found in the last of Soloviev's works in which the author considered all of human history to be a failure.[69]

Once a week, Alexander stocked up on books provided him by Nikolai Pestov, a professor of chemistry. In those times, people never really knew whom they should suspect. If someone rang at the door while Pestov already had a visitor, he would have the visitor come into another room. Alexander saw a photo of St. Theresa of Lisieux on Pestov's desk, as well as images of Catholic saints on the wall. It seems that Pestov had been converted through his contacts with Baptists, and he helped Alexander learn about Western Christianity.[70]

Along with his secular studies, Alexander threw himself into theology and began to read the Fathers of the Church. In order to better understand the Bible, he studied Roman antiquity, especially the ancient Orient. In his work on biblical history, Alexander was encouraged by Boris Vassiliev, who supported his ambition of reconciling scientific knowledge and faith.[71] Mother Maria also approved his desire to consecrate himself to biblical studies.[72] He began, always on his own initiative, the systematic study of the subjects in the seminary's curriculum.

At the same age, he also began to be an acolyte in the parish of the Nativity of St. John the Baptist,[73] to do readings, and to sing in the choir. For a westerner, this activity may seem rather ordinary, but serving in the Orthodox liturgy requires considerably more knowledge than is required for an altar boy in a Catholic parish. What is more, that a teenager in the USSR should be an acolyte is one of the paradoxes of the time. Somewhat later on, Alexander was to have a companion in this service; he was a young seminarian from Zagorsk who subsequently became a bishop under the name of Philaret. He is now the head of the Byelorussian Orthodox Church.[74]

Alexander began to write at a very early age. At twelve he wrote an article on nature and a play on St. Francis of Assisi.[75] He wrote his first theological essay when only fifteen, which was no doubt merely a school assignment. It contained, however, the structure of all his subsequent works.[76]

In 1953, some months before Stalin died, Alexander finished high school. Seeing that he had already assimilated the whole seminary curriculum on his own, he decided to go to university. Stalin's last years were marked by a vast anti-Semitic campaign which, because of Alexander's Jewish origins, blocked his access to university. He therefore decided to go to the Moscow Fur Institute where he could give himself over to his passion- biology.

Once admitted to the institute, he continued to pursue his theological studies on his own by reading the prescribed texts in the academy's program. He began to write a short history of the Church and then composed his first really complete book: What is the Bible Talking About and What Does it Teach Us? At this time, Alexander became a close friend of Fr. Nicholas Golubtsov,[77] who was himself a former parishioner of the Mechev priests and who was serving in a Moscow parish. He was a well-educated man, having done his studies in biology with several brothers and sisters in monastic orders. To Alexander, they all resembled the heroes of Dostoevsky. Fr. Nicholas had an open spirit and could talk easily to unbelievers. He represented fo Alexander the same priestly ideal as had Fr. Seraphim, as he remembered him through the stories of his mother and her cousin. Alexander chose Fr. Nicholas as his spiritual father.[78]

The institute was closed in 1955, and the students were transferred to a school in Irkutsk, Siberia. Alexander spent three years here. To his former activities he now added such practical tasks as observing animals in the forests of Siberia. The students were interested in their area of study, and the relations between them were quite friendly.

While still in his first year at the institute in Moscow, during a boring course, Alexander had read a a "brick" by Fr. Florensky on the Church- a book he had cut up, page by page, so as not to be noticed. His fellow students did not know exactly what the book was all about but did not seem to mind. Seeing that Alexander was a good classmate who participated in all their activities, they had no problem with the fact that he was interested in "advanced studies." After all, he had the right to have a hobby like everyone else. He took a few fellow students into his confidence in his second year. The others suspected that he had religious ideas, and many believed him to be a Buddhist. In his third year, the whole class knew that he was Orthodox. After he arrived in Irkutsk, Alexander met the bishop[79] and began to do various jobs for him. He openly ran between the institute and the church, which were just across from each other, and his fellow students saw nothing in this to find fault with. Remembereing this period, Fr. Alexander said later: "imagine what would have hap-

ALEXANDER AROUND 1955

GLEB YAKUNIN WITH HIS MOTHER AROUND 1950

pened if, on the first day at the institute, I had begun to make the sign of the cross in an ostentatious way for everyone to see! They had to be brought to understand, little by little, that someone like themselves could be a believer."

During his first year at Irkutsk, Alexander shared a small apartment with Gleb Yakunin, who was later on to become a priest and one of the eminent figures in the struggle for religious liberty. Gleb had been raised by a very loving and believing mother. One morning at the age of fourteen, when his mother and aunts got him up to take him to communion, he told them categorically, "Do what you want to me, but I am not going." From that moment on, he felt himself to be a convinced atheist. In Irkutsk, he began slowly to shake off the Soviet ideology and to search for a philosophy of life. Up to that time, the only believers Gleb had met were old women- very good women, but not very well educated. His contact with Alexander contributed to his progressive return to the faith.[80]

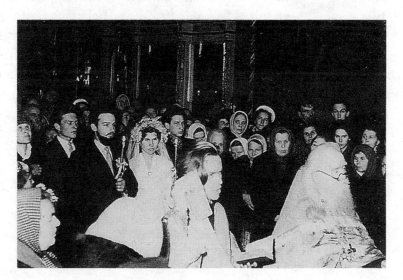

ALEXANDER'S WEDDING

KHRUSHCHEV BETWEEN TWO COSMONAUTS

The Beginnings of Priesthood

CHAPTER 5

NEAR FR. SERAPHIM'S GRAVE AROUND 1955

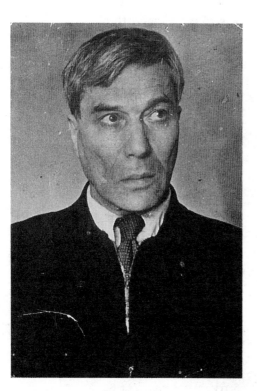

BORIS PASTERNAK   ALEXANDER SOLZHENITSYN

In February 1956, the Communist party held its 20th congress, during which Khrushchev secretly read his famous report on Stalin's crimes. In the weeks that followed the congress, the contents of this report slowly spread throughout the country. As a result, a whole world view collapsed. Three years before, the people had mourned Stalin's passing; he had been the greatest genius of all time and of all peoples, having been deified as no Roman emperor, no Pharaoh, no oriental despot had ever been. Many children considered him to be their best friend and really thought he was immortal. Now this same man was reduced to the level of a scoundrel. Millions of men and women were freed from the gulag. Solzhenitsyn, still a complete unknown, was among the freed prisoners. After several years in the camps, he had been sentenced to life in the Kazakhstan desert. Under the guidance of Rudenko, the new attorney general of the USSR, the whole judicial system was overhauled. Censorship was relaxed, and contacts with the outside world were re-established. This period of history has come to be called "the Thaw": the ice pack broke up and started to move, though it had not yet melted. Even though Khrushchev had ended the cult of Stalin and the reign of mass terror, he had no intention of doing away with the Soviet system. On the contrary, he hoped to restore it to its ideological militancy by returning to "Leninist norms". What is more, several months after the 20th congress, the Hungarian revolt against the Communist government was drowned in blood by Soviet tanks. In 1958, the party called the intellectuals to order by launching a mud-slinging campaign against Boris Pasternak; he had just won the Nobel prize in literature for a novel he had dared to publish abroad whose main character expressed doubts about the Revolution. Nonetheless, some small amount of freedom of speech, the awakening to the horrors of Stalinism, and the return of former prisoners provoked a certain excitement in society. The whole country began to join in debate and discussion. In Moscow, meetings of young people gathering to hear poetry readings on Mayakovsky Place took a political turn. The first typed magazines, later called samizdat, began to appear, carried under people's coats. Something that looked like independent public opinion began to take shape in the capital.

The moral atmosphere of the country began to evolve. Popular books of the time were quite indicative of the trend, even if their literary quality was negligible; they dealt with "sincerity", alluded to the refusal of individuals to continue to be simply "cogs of a wheel", and affirmed that "man does not live by bread alone".

There was then the beginning of a return to values that furiously had been buried after the Revolution. Nadia Mandelstam, the widow of the great Russian poet Osip Mandelstam who disappeared in the gulag, recalled this period in her memoirs, in which she analyzed the evolution of thinking in Russia throughout the twentieth century. A generation had passed, and the new one was less terrorized. Its members could not be convinced that their fathers' acts were just; they no longer believed that everything was possible.[81]

One of Solzhenitsyn's heroes denounced the following terrible verses that children recited at school: "We have too long loved;

we finally want to hate", saying: "The opposite is what they should have learned. To hell with your hatred! When all is said and done, we want to love! This is what socialism should be like." [82] Such rethinking, which continued to develop as time went on, was then only in its initial stages.

The famous saying could no longer be uttered, "You can't make an omelet without breaking some eggs." People still believed, however, in the possibility of making a Communist omelet, that is, of building a Communist society. The young people of Mayakovsky Place thought that the only thing they needed to do to achieve such a goal was to get rid of the remnants of Stalinism and restore the "purity" of Lenin and his companions. Solzhenitsyn's hero went even further by talking about "moral socialism". One way or the other, people were dreaming of "a communism with a human face", as advocated by the leaders of the 1968 Prague Spring.

Believers also felt the first effects of de-Stalinization and witnessed the return from the gulag of many churchmen, physically exhausted by their trials and often with little time left to enjoy their newly-found freedom. Fr. Ieraks moved into a little house in Vladimir and died in 1959. Fr. Piotr Shipkov found the strength to take on a parish and even to repair his church before dying the same year. Bishop Afanassy lived a little longer, until 1962, but the civil authorities would not even allow him to celebrate the liturgy in a local church. [83]

Unlike the rest of the society, the Church did not profit long from the Thaw. In 1958, the Communist party decided to launch a vigorous antireligious campaign. Khrushchev soon announced that the building of a Communist society would take about another twenty years; in the meantime, it was obvious that all religion would have to disappear.

As a result, an avalanche of antireligious propaganda fell on the country. The *Journal of the Moscow Patriarchate* then subscribed to a special press service that regularly sent it all the articles having to do with religion. The workers in this service must have begged for mercy, for each day there were so many articles denouncing religion that it was literally impossible to collect them all together. For the first time since the war, a new antireligious journal appeared: *Science and Religion*. Millions of antireligious pamphlets and books were published. One of the first such publications, written by a former seminary professor, was entitled *Why I Stopped Believing in God.* In the prevailing climate, many priests renounced heir faith, and the press naturally got a lot of mileage from these defections and renunciations.

Half the churches were closed. The local authorities often carried out these operations with great brutality, breaking everything that they found inside. There were as many as one hundred fifty church closings a day.[84] The priests who were thus deprived of their parishes, without any other source of income to support a family, were often reduced to begging. The number of monastic communities was drastically reduced. There had been about one hundred after the war, but now only sixteen were left. Five seminaries were liquidated. Only those in Moscow, Leningrad and Odessa remained open, along with the two theological academies in Moscow and Leningrad.

The authorities arrested and tried some churchmen, but preferred to use administrative methods against the Church by invoking security measures, urbanization plans, sanitation problems, etc., and by putting pressure on the Patriarchate and the clergy. They took special care to see that nearly all the bishops were rotated.[85]

A thinly veiled reference was made to these procedures in a confidential report written some years later, and leaked to the public. The report dealt specifically with monasteries, but the same situation existed for churches:

> "Following the orders of the governing authorities, an immense work has been accomplished here locally with the intention of reducing the number of monasteries. To this end, the growing influence of the Council for the Affairs of the Russian Orthodox Church on the Patriarchate and the bishops has been put to good use. Several dozen monasteries have been closed by the churchmen themselves. In 1963, the Monastery of the Kiev Caves, which attracted as many as five hundred thousand pilgrims a year, was closed on the false pretense that the ground was giving way in the caves. It was therefore claimed that studies of the soil had to be made and restoration work carried out.[86]

The Patriarch was an old man who in 1957 had celebrated his eightieth birthday, and whose secretary protected him from all outside contacts. The Patriarch's second in command, Bishop Nikolai,[87] nonetheless tried to react. He had been the main architect of the policy of compromise between Church and State after 1945, hoping that the Church would profit in return; Bishop Nikolai gave himself entirely over to promoting the image of the USSR throughout the world, to the point that he was sometimes called "the second minister of foreign affairs". He also knew how to appeal to the patriotism of Russian emigres in hopes of getting them to return to the Soviet Union.

The new antireligious offensive meant the failure of his efforts. Bishop Nikolai succeeded however, in persuading the Patriarch to take advantage of a peace conference in Moscow to which he had been invited, to allude to the attacks on the Church and then to excommunicate apostates. The civil authorities were watching though, and put pressure on the patriarch to dismiss Bishop Nikolai. He died some months later, abandoned by everybody.[88]

The Soviet government decided to put the 1929 law on religious associations into full effect again. Now it must not be forgotten that the Church regulations concerning parish organization adopted by the 1945 council openly contradicted the old civil law. The council on the Affairs of the Russian Orthodox Church demanded that the Church harmonize its statute with the civil legislation. Finally, as a result the Patriarchate invited the bishops to come celebrate the feast of St. Sergius at Zagorsk on July 18, 1961. Without any prior announcement, the bishops were called to a meeting after the ceremony and forced quickly to approve the change in Church law. Henceforth, parish administration was again in the hands of a committee of three laymen having sole responsibility for parish affairs. Priests were to be concerned only with liturgical celebrations; they were reduced to the level of salaried employees in charge of religious services. The civil power was quite able to ensure that its people sat on the parish committees; such flunkies could themselves then close the churches. The 1961 episcopal assembly had not been convoked in a regular fashion, and the new law was contrary to the traditional organization of the Church. One bishop undertook various measures to attempt to annul this decision. This Bishop Germogen,[89] a man of great bearing, was a true "prince of the Church". He had been a student of Fr. Florensky at the Moscow Theological Academy before the Revolution. Ordained by Patriarch Tikhon, he had been made the higumen of the Monastery of the Kiev Caves, and was then sent to the gulag for ten years. In 1956 he became the Bishop of Tashkent in Uzbekistan. There he was very firm and refused to have any of the churches in his diocese closed. He was even able to enlarge his cathedral. This made him very popular with the

BISHOP GERMOGEN

FR. DIMITRI DUDKO

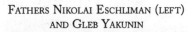

ANATOLI LEVITIN

FATHERS NIKOLAI ESCHLIMAN (LEFT)
AND GLEB YAKUNIN

faithful, but ultimately cost him his job; he was soon removed and remained without a diocese for some time.

The other bishops were resigned to the change, feeling that any resistance was useless anyway. One bishop confided one day:

> "I often wonder if we are right in keeping quiet and not publicly denouncing what is happening in the Church and the difficulties it has to deal with. Sometimes I am completely disgusted by the whole affair; I just want to abandon everything and go into retirement. My conscience makes me feel guilty for not retiring, but then again my conscience tells me that I must not abandon the faithful or the Church. For to denounce or even just openly to criticize the functioning of the Church would mean, in the best of situations, being forbidden from any kind of Church activity. In any case, protesting would change nothing."[90]

It was at just this time in 1961 that Yuri Gagarin became the first man to go into space. This feat was supposed to show the definitive triumph of Soviet technology and science. What is more, the Russian cosmonaut brought back irrefutable proof that God did not exist: Gagarin said that he had not met God in space! The same year, the 22nd congress of the Party adopted a new program that sought to intensify the building of Communism; paradoxically, at the same time this congress marked the beginning of a new stage in the de-Stalinization process. The speeches against Stalin's methods were so virulent that when Solzhenitsyn read them, he decided to come out of the shadows and to try to publish his novel on the camps, *A Day in the Life of Ivan Denisovich*. He was, in fact, able to publish it in 1962.

The intellectuals, however, did not raise a finger to defend the Church even though the protest movement was taking form among them, a movement that would later give birth to a real dissidence movement and to the struggle for human rights. The intellectuals did not ignore the Church through cowardice, indifference, or complicity. It had been so well closed up in its ghetto, so well isolated from society, that they were not even aware that the Church was suffering repression. Only a few isolated people raised their voices publicly to denounce the antireligious campaign and the closing of churches and monasteries. Credit goes especially to Anatoli Levitin,[91] whose virulent articles against the apostates appeared in the samizdat press. A very colorful character who had been attracted to the Church since childhood, Levitin had been ordained a deacon by the leader of the renovators and was almost the only advocate in his country of a system that tried to reconcile socialism and Christianity. He had hardly been released from the gulag when his boldness got him sent right back.

Another response, circulated in the samizdat press in reply to a priest's public renunciation of the faith, was made by a Fr. Zheludkov.[92] The civil authorities in Pskov, where he lived, revoked his permission to celebrate the liturgy because of his protest. Like Levitin, he had made contacts with the renovators in his teenage years because of a hope for a profound reform of the Church, rather than because of any support for the political tactics of the group. Anxious to enter into dialogue with non-believers and "anonymous Christians", Fr. Zheludkov was to become well known in the following decade.

Paradoxically, at the very moment when society was showing its ignorance of the Church's situation and the persecutions it was undergoing, the moral quest, which had appeared after the start of the de-Stalinization program, began to open up to religious questions. Certain people became believers, and some were even baptized. The number of such people was obviously very small, but their conversions marked a total break with the general cultural atmosphere, the convictions of their peer group, and their education. These people had entered school when atheism reigned supreme. In their families and among their friends and associates, believing in God was about as ridiculous and absurd as thinking that the earth was flat. Svetlana Alliluyeva became a convert at this period and noted the following:

"I remember very well the spring and summer of 1961 in Moscow. I was thirty-five years old. I was tormented by an inner anxiety that nothing seemed to be able to ease. I had no interest in church services, books, or icons. They said nothing to me, but I already knew several persons my age who had been baptized. I thought of them with surprise and respect."

One day, Svetlana had a discussion about suicide with Siniavsky,[93] a specialist in Russian literature who wrote novels in secret and was to have them published abroad one day under a pseudonym. For this action, he was condemned to a long prison term after a highly publicized trial in 1966. Siniavsky explained to Svetlana that by committing suicide, people believe that they are eliminating themselves but, in fact, they only kill their bodies because the souls belong to God, the sole Master of life. Instead of attaining freedom, people who commit suicide are guilty of a terrible sin.

This conversation was a revelation for Svetlana because Siniavsky had formulated a new idea that she was just beginning to understand. "Thou shalt not kill" is the essential law of human conduct on earth. Life is eternal and immense; any attack against it is a great crime. Svetlana began to read the psalms. She re-read Tolstoy and Dostoevsky from a completely new point of view. In the spring of 1962 she asked to be baptized. She was Stalin's own daughter!

Siniavsky put Svetlana in touch with Fr. Nikolai Golubtsov, who had himself baptized Siniavsky (and who was, it must be remembered, Fr. Alexander Men's spiritual father). The first encounter with Fr. Nikolai left Svetlana very moved. She did not know how to act. She had never met a priest before and was struck by his simplicity, as well as by the time and attention he gave to each parishioner who came to talk with him after the liturgy.[94]

When the antireligious offensive was launched, Alexander Men was about to finish his studies at Irkutsk. As was normal, he planned to work in his field for three years after finishing the institute, in order to obtain his final certification. Following that, he was to enter the seminary at Zagorsk as planned. At the moment when final exams were beginning, however, he was suddenly excluded on the pretext that he had not taken some required courses. In fact, the institute had finally learned about his relations with the local bishop. He had to leave without any diploma whatsoever. He took the news as a sign for him to get on with his real vocation. Having returned to Moscow, his decision was confirmed by Fr. Nikolai Golubtsov, who gave Alexander his blessing. Anatoli Vedernikov, who had participated in the reorganization of the seminary after the war, was then editorial secretary of the *Journal of the Moscow Patriarchate*; he made things easy for Alexander. Vedernikov introduced Alexander to a vicar bishop of the Moscow diocese[95] who immediately appreciated the young man's talents and ordained him a deacon on Pentecost Sunday, July 1, 1958 in the church of Fr. Nikolai Golubtsov, despite the fact that he had not even started seminary. He was sent to a parish near Moscow, near Odintsovo.[96] Here he stayed for two years. The living conditions were hard. He received a miserable salary and had to live with his wife and their one-year-old daughter in a dilapidated house. The inside wall between the floor and the window was covered with a thick layer of ice that did not melt until the end of winter. There were very few parishioners. As for the priest, a former accountant, the liturgy consisted above all in the most scrupulous following of all the rubrics, and it was not impossible that right in the middle of a service, he would begin singing a part the choir had forgotten. The service would stop dead while the terrified choir members frantically looked for their parts. Despite the atmosphere, it was in this church that the young Fr. Deacon Alexander began his first series of lectures on the life of Christ. During this time, he took correspondence courses from the Leningrad seminary.

On September 1, 1960, Alexander was ordained priest by another vicar bishop of Moscow, a man known for his prayer and his deep spirituality.[97] The ceremony took place in the Donskoi Monastery where Patriarch Tikhon had lived and where he was buried. Fr. Alexander was sent as a second priest to a parish about thirty miles from Moscow in a town called Alabino.[98] After about a year there he became the pastor. In the middle of the persecutions of the Khrushchev era, his little parish was a sort of haven on which the 1961 reforms had little effect. In contrast to parishes elsewhere, whose councils were most often controlled by the party, the *starosta*[99] of Fr. Alexander's parish was completely devoted to him. With his sense of human relations, Fr. Alexander succeeded in establishing the best relations with the city authorities, and the parish and city hall were able to do favors for each other.

The church was in bad repair, and the iconostasis and wall paintings were in an abominable style. Fr. Alexander undertook a whole program of repairs and restoration. He even had new icons painted. He asked an artist to repaint the walls in the style of a great painter of the nineteenth century: the style of ancient icons was foreign to the people, who did not understand it and preferred affected and "edifying" naturalism. It was not possible to change everything overnight; popular habits could only be changed little by little. The candle desk was put in the vestibule of the church so that the liturgy would not be disturbed by the noise of clinking coins. There were grounds around the church, a small house with a room for receiving visitors, and a house for the priest's family, which had a new member -a son. In his free moments Fr. Alexander went out into the church garden to write his books. Thanks to Anatoli Vedernikov, he published about twenty articles in the *Journal of the Moscow Patriarchate*, which got him the honor of being attacked in *Science and Religion*.[100] Fr. Alexander was soon assisted by a young priest friend of his.[101] Every Saturday he explained the creed, the meaning of the principal prayers, and of the liturgy. Some young converts came to him; many stayed for a long time. With these people, a little community of active Christians began to take shape. They humorously nicknamed the place "the abbey".

After the war, priests had been permitted to celebrate private services in people's homes, especially at the time of death, and for special prayers in the cemeteries. Now, during the antireligious campaign begun in 1958, such practices were forbidden by secret governmental instructions. The priest had to obtain a prior authorization for each case from the local authorities, who only occasionally approved such requests. Fr. Alexander, however, continued to go to people's homes and to the cemeteries for memorial services, giving a sermon each time. Circumstances had worked in his favor because, when a member of a civil servant's family had died, he had been given the necessary authorization, though only as a special measure. Using this as a precedent, he asked that the permission be renewed--two hundred and fifty times! The parish still had a car, which fact distinguished Fr.

IN BACK YARD OF THE ABBEY

Alexander's church from other parishes, whose cars hd been confiscated; Fr. Alexander was thus able to use this means of transportation to visit his parishioners within a twenty mile radius.

Unfortunately, the abbey was soon to be destroyed through the fault of one man whom Fr. Alexander, in order to help him and at the recommendation of a friend, had engaged as a reader. In Orthodox practice, it is a wide-spread custom to give a layman the permanent position of reader for the good order of the services.[102] This man was pleasant but a bit crazy, and he liked to drink. He had the unfortunate idea of taking Fr. Alexander and some of his friends to the museum in Istra where he worked. However, he just could not resist the temptation of going out for a drink during the visit. He made a spectacle of himself, drawing the attention of his boss, a fanatical atheist who liked to amuse himself by drawing pictures on icons, burning out the eyes on the faces, and making tabernacles into waste baskets. To make matters worse, the alcoholic reader had some time before brought Fr. Alexander a few old books. Since they had no stamp, no registration, there was nothing to indicate that they had been stolen.

The day after the excursion, the police and the KGB arrived at the abbey along with the museum's director. The search and seizure operation lasted all day. Seeing Fr. Alexander's library, all his theology books and foreign language journals, the director was beside himself with joy. As he told his companions, "We came here by chance, and we have obviously caught ourselves a very big fish!" A local paper published a satirical article on this "affair". The authorities, in the middle of the antireligious campaign, decided to make a federal case out of the matter. The file went up to Rudenko himself, the attorney general of the USSR. Fr. Alexander had to undergo a long interrogation. Against all expectation, experts evaluated the books at no more than fifty rubles, the excitement quickly died down, and the file was closed.

Following on the heels of the book affair, Fr. Alexander was involved in another story about church repairs which were to be paid for "under the table", according to the wide-spread practice in the USSR, a practice which it was impossible to avoid if certain kinds of work were to be carried out at all. The authorities threatened to implicate Fr. Alexander, so he decided to take advantage of his vacation in the summer of 1964 to see the world 'without waiting to be forced to do so behind bars', as he humorously said later. He and his wife went on a Volga cruise, from which he was brusquely recalled by a telegram from his friends. He had been summoned by the head of the Council for the Affairs of the Orthodox Church in the Moscow area, a high-ranking official of the KGB.[103] This official ran Fr. Alexander through the wringer, repeating the same question fifty times: "What are we going to do with you?" He finally forbade Fr. Alexander to serve.

A second time, everything unexpectedly worked out. The anti-religious offensive, in the form that Khrushchev had given it, tapered off. The last act of the frenzy seems to have been the destruction that summer[104] of the Church of the Transfiguration, in the heart of Moscow, with a mass of the faithful gathered inside. The wind suddenly began to shift. Khrushchev's authority in the party was increasingly questioned and undermined, and his adversaries secretly prepared to eliminate him. A meeting of the Council of the Affairs of the Orthodox Church was held at that very moment: was a new tactic adopted? Did the Council members receive new instructions? Whatever really happened, the head of the Moscow region lost interest in his "guilty party" after this meeting, asking no more than that he leave Alabino. Fr. Alexander was nonetheless able to celebrate the liturgy for the Dormition of the Virgin on August 15/28th.[105] Then, with the help of the diocesan secretary, Fr. Alexander was able to find a vacant post as vicar in a parish near Tarasovka[106], north of Moscow towards Zagorsk. He was immediately given the position. As with his previous parishes, this church was named for the Protection of the Virgin.

Fr. Alexander escaped without any scars, but the abbey had lived out its time. Never again would conditions be as favorable as they had been at Alabino. At Tarasovka he did not even have a place to receive his parishioners; he could only meet and talk with them outside or on the train.

During the time the abbey existed, there was also a circle of young priests in and around Moscow who were fired up by the desire to renew the Church. There were about a dozen of them. Besides Fr. Alexander, the best known were Frs. Yakunin, Dudko, and Eschliman.

After his studies in Irkutsk, Gleb Yakunin had continued to seek his vocation; he became a reader in a Moscow church and was finally ordained. Being driven by a highly developed sense of justice, Fr. Gleb had the temperament of a fighter.

Fr. Dimitri Dudko had already been through the camps. He was the son of peasants and had seen the horrors of collectivization. In Fr. Dimitri's youth, when government agents broke into the family izba, his father, sleeping on the only sack of flour they had, cried: "No, no! My children will die of hunger!" The men roughed up the old man and took the sack After the war, Dimitri entered the seminary. In 1948, he was arrested for having written a poem judged "anti-Soviet", and sent to the gulag. Freed in 1956, he returned to Moscow and finished his studies at the seminary; after a long wait he was ordained priest, and then went to a parish in the capital. He was a simple man who knew how to touch the hearts of his parishioners.

Fr. Nikolai Eschliman, on the other hand, had an aristocratic background and was married to the granddaughter of one of Nicholas II's ministers. Brilliant, and a gifted painter and musician, he had studied in a school of design. Fr. Nikolai came to the faith late in life, and had known Bishop Pimen, who was later to succeed Alexei I as Patriarch but who at the time had only recently become a bishop. Bishop Pimen took Nikolai under his wing, encouraged him to become a priest, and ordained him.[107]

Fr. Alexander suggested to them that they organize regular meetings to deepen their theological knowledge together, to share their experience as priests, and to try to resolve common pastoral problems. But the conditions in which the 1961 reform had just been adopted provoked a real malaise among the clergy. The priests felt as though the bishops had abandoned them. This isolation was particularly hard for Fr. Alexander to bear. He once noted that"the bishop is the successor of the Apostles, and we priests are only his helpers." So in his own name and that of his friends, Fr. Alexander wrote a letter to Bishop Germogen[108] which essentially said the following: 'We know about your courageous position; we know that you resisted attempts to close churches and that you have never accepted the 1961 reforms. Even though we are not part of your diocese and are not under your authority, we ask you to be our spiritual bishop and allow us to speak with you when we have a problem.' Bishop Germogen gave a favorable response to the letter and came to Alabino.

At that very moment, news arrived in Moscow concerning the Pochaev Monastery in the Ukraine, where the authorities were subjecting the monks to every kind of persecution. They had cut off the water, the heat, and the electricity of the monastery; they had confiscated the monks' papers; the monks were insulted, put in asylums, and beat up. One of the monks had been tortured to death. Another had been beaten, gagged, forcibly dragged away and never seen again.[109] The monks had written letters abroad asking for help. Later on it became normal to appeal to international opinion, but at the time this was something new. Copies of these letters fell by accident into the hands of Fr. Alexander and his friends, who were very touched by them. They were written clumsily, by men unused to writing. The young priests felt that it was their duty to gather all the facts together and to present them in a proper form so that public opinion could be alerted. They decided to talk over their idea with Levitin, whom they often invited to their meetings and who had done everything he could to defend the Pochaev monks. They came to the conclusion that they had to go further, right to the root of the problem: the passivity of the bishops and the famous 1961 reform. The priests also consulted Anatoli Vedernikov, and conceived the idea of writing a letter to be read to the Patriarch in the cathedral. Frs. Alexander and Dimitri were firm about doing nothing without episcopal approval, so Bishop Germogen was made aware of their project and approved it. Levitin brought a proposed text that was judged too excessive. Fr. Alexander wrote one that many thought, on the contrary, to be too moderate. The plan was then put off for a time. In the meantime, Khrushchev was removed on October 14, 1964, and his expulsion gave rise to hopes for a change in policy. The project of writing a letter to the Patriarch was now set in a different context, and Bishop Germogen and Vedernikov no longer thought it was the right thing to do. Things dragged on without any decision. So in November and December of 1965, on their own, Frs. Yakunin and Eschliman signed two letters denouncing the innumerable intrusions of the State in the affairs of the Church, addressing one to Patriarch Alexei I and the other to the head of State.[110]

The action caused quite a sensation among the clergy and was welcomed by many parish priests. The Patriarch reacted in a contradictory manner. On the one hand, despite the authors' virulence against the hierarchy, the submission of the bishops to the dictates of the State, and "bad pastors", the Patriarch confided to his entourage that the priests were right. On the other hand, he accused them of wanting to get him in trouble with the civil authorities. One bishop stated in private that life was, after all, worth living. Bishop Pimen, who had become Metropolitan of Krutitsy, responsible for the Moscow diocese and the Patriarch's right-hand man, called to two priests to account. He reproached Fr. Eschliman for having done him an evil turn, and said that 'a wall could not be broken down by having people butt their heads against it'. There was, finally, no real dialogue between the priests and the hierarchy, and as could have been expected, the Patriarch suspended them. Once the dust from the matter settled, it was obvious that the initiative of Frs. Yakunin and Eschliman provoked no movement inside the Church, despite their hopes.

Thanks to his strong constitution, Fr. Yakunin overcame his discouragement and carried on the fight for religious liberty. Although Fr. Eschliman had all the gifts that would have made him a remarkable pastor, he sank into despondency. He came under the influence of a strange person, leading to the dissolution of the small group of priests that had been so united at the beginning, despite their differences. The father of this bizarre individual was one of the chiefs of the secret police and had even named his son Felix in honor of its founder. The father was himself shot in 1937. After the war, Felix was recruited as an informer. Ordered to infiltrate a clandestine yoga group, he was converted to their ideas and announced that he no longer wanted to be a spy. Everyone was arrested. In the gulag, Felix was suspected of being an informer. One day when his fellow prisoners uncovered a real informer, Felix was forced to stab him to death in order to prove that he was not himself a traitor. Having become a believer during his detention, impassioned and living in expectation of the imminent end of the world, he could exert a certain fascination, especially over young converts.

The impact made by the two letters was not limited to Church circles, and finally attracted the attention of the newly-formed dissident groups to the Church's situation. Solzhenitsyn was impressed and even inspired by the courage of the two priests:

"In the spring of 1966, I read with admiration the protests of the two priests, Eschliman and Yakunin. Theirs was a pure and courageous voice, full of integrity, which was raised to defend a Church which had never known how to defend itself, did not know how to defend itself, and, what is more, did not want to defend itself. I read the letters and I envied the authors. I had not dared to protest, and my lack of action worked on me no doubt, silently and unconsciously. And then, with the sudden clarity of infallible decisions, I understood that I too had to do something like what they did."[111]

Finally, the two letters drew a lot of attention abroad, where they contributed to the development of a campaign in support of Russian Christians.

It was often said and believed that the two letters were written by Fr. Alexander, and that was why he was suspected by the authorities. He admired the courage of the two priests and appreciated the moral significance of their action,[112] but it seems he regretted that they appeared to be a dissident movement inside the Church. He did not interpret the word *dissident* to mean the same thing it meant in the USSR of the seventies, that is, opposition to the Soviet regime, but rather in the etymological sense of a break within the ecclesial community and, under the circumstances, of a break with the episcopate. Fr. Alexander wanted to concentrate on interior work: on the work of evangelization, on pastoral activity in the parishes to benefit the faithful and those who were searching. He considered his mission to lie elsewhere: in answering the spiritual aspirations then coming to the surface in the society. And it was precisely in 1966 that many people, young and not so young, suddenly began to come to him. In his new parish he witnessed, as he said later, the "first demographic explosion".

If we lift up our eyes, we will already see the fields becoming covered with golden ears of grain. "The harvest is plentiful", the Scriptures say, "but the laborers are few."[113]

The Brezhnev Years

CHAPTER 6

L. Brezhnev

Andrei Sakharov

Patriarch Pimen

Khrushchev was forced from power by a palace revolution. The members of the party establishment owed their physical security to him: they no longer had to fear, as under Stalin, being awakened in the night by a knock at the door, to be sent off to prison with only a little bundle of clothes, but they felt threatened with the loss of their job because of a new reform prepared by their impetuous boss. They also feared that, in the end, the helter-skelter initiatives of Number One, especially the de-Stalinization program he started, might end up putting the whole system in danger. Even Khrushchev sensed the impending danger because, just before his fall, he had already begun to try to halt the process. Brezhnev, however, incarnated the hopes of this entire caste, called the Nomenclatura, which more than anything else needed political stability in order to secure their privileges. It seems that certain "conspirators" against Khrushchev wanted to return to a pure, strict form of Communism, but a simple return to Stalin's methods would also have endangered the tranquillity of the Nomenclatura. Stalin's crimes were no longer denounced in the Brezhnev era, but he was only partially rehabilitated, and in a cringing way at that.

The most spectacular sign of the end of the Thaw was the heavy sentences given in February 1966 to Andrei Siniavsky and Yuli Daniel, writers accused of publishing their works abroad under pseudonyms. Strangely enough, this first big political trial since

Stalin's death also marked the first visible manifestation of public opinion. Not only did the accused writers refuse to plead guilty, but they received the support of a petition-writing campaign that gathered hundreds of signatures from throughout the country. The new governing regime tried to put the socialist camp back in order by crushing the 1968 Prague Spring by means of a massive military operation. The curtain had fallen on the impossible "Communism with a human face." The abandoning of the de-Stalinization program and the invasion of Czechoslovakia put an end to the hopes for change born after the 20th congress. A formless discontent, passive but massive, was rising in the country; it was aimed however, more at the difficulties of daily life than at the regime itself.

The people were losing faith in the official ideology, though no one really noticed. They had lived for years on the promise of an earthly paradise, fed to them by Communist propaganda; all their energies had been mobilized for the building of a future, collectivized, Communist society. As time went on, however, the ordinary citizen stopped looking toward this radiant future, which seemed to be moving farther and farther away, instead of getting closer and closer. The result was that the rights of the individual began to take priority over those of the collective.

Right from the start of Brezhnev's tenure in office, the ideological leaders worried about the skepticism and nihilism of the younger generation, who knew about the great feats of the Soviet people only through movies. Brezhnev was soon to become aware of just how true this was. The propaganda machine regularly denounced the attraction of jeans and rock music for the young. The party bitterly protested against self-centeredness, the lack of professionalism, and the passion for acquisition and accumulation.

The whole society showed a desire to take possession of its past once again, to find its roots and traditions, and to get reconnected to the historical continuity that had been broken by the Bolshevik Revolution. Suddenly there appeared an interest in ancient Russian art with its icons and religious architecture. The authorities tried to channel this interest and to use it to their own ends by creating the Association for the Protection of Historical Monuments, which in no time counted millions of members.

Literature also promoted a new type of hero: in place of the statues of the builders of the future set up in public places, their muscles taut and their bodies stretching out to the future, there were substituted those of humble men and women, peasants who formerly had been treated with contempt as "survivors" at the end of a miserable life, the last remnants of a civilization swallowed up by collectivization. This new literary type had been introduced by Solzhenitsyn when he was still being published inside the USSR before Khrushchev's fall, and was developed throughout the whole Brezhnev period. The heroine of *The House of Matryona* was a model of humility, self-denial, and charity. According to the conclusion of the story, this poor woman to whom no one paid any attention was, as the proverb says, "the righteous person without whom no village can exist, nor any city, nor even our whole world".

While the writers who illustrated this theme were able to publish their books in the USSR, a whole parallel culture developed in restricted circles on the edge of the official culture, with its own clandestine network: the *samizdat* printed and circulated writings from within, while the *tamizdat*[114] smuggled Russian books into the country; the *magnitizdat* recorded and distributed politically loaded songs, first on tape and then on cassettes; paintings were shown in private apartments, and concerts as well as films were presented in the clubs of institutes having a restricted membership.

Finally the dissidence movement took off. It was by no means an organized movement pursuing a precise goal; rather it was made up of individuals who claimed the right to think in their own way. These individuals gave themselves a name which, for lack of a better translation, can be rendered as *dissidents*. They were men and women who one day decided to transgress the code of conduct imposed by the regime.

In reality, the Soviet person was encouraged to live in a constant state of vigilance. He constantly had to watch himself, to censure himself, to keep himself in check.[115] This mechanism of "doublethink" had already been described with clinical precision by the English writer Orwell:

> *"Doublethink* means the power of holding two contradictory beliefs in one's mind simultaneously, and accepting both of them. ...to use conscious deception while retaining the firmness of purpose that goes with complete honesty. To tell deliberate lies while genuinely believing in them..."[116]

The Communist regime aimed at getting total submission from its subjects, and the sign of submission was the support and use of the official party line. In reality, it is very difficult to speak when a person's deep inner self is disconnected from what he is saying. Such a mental schism naturally causes a psychological tension that is nearly unbearable. In Brezhnev's time, the tension brought on by "doublespeak" was somewhat reduced, due to the fact that the government's propaganda machine kept piling up more and more empty statements that had no direct impact on people's lives. This also explains why the official norms had little hold on the population. Nonetheless, citizens had to continue repeating what they heard in the media and at political meetings, but in order to get over the gulf between what they said in public and what they thought in private, citizens had to compromise with the ideology and try to believe certain statements of the propaganda. In other words, they had to adjust what they were thinking to what they were saying.

The dissidents, however, took the opposite path, deciding to speak and act as they thought. In so doing, they could not escape from being slowly but surely caught up in the grinding gears of official repression. They had to endure problems at work; anonymous telephone calls in the night; threats; men in black cars in front of their buildings, watching all day long; being tailed, interrogated and undergoing search-and-seizure operations. This lonely combat between one individual and the enormous repressive machinery of the USSR required extraordinary willpower. Such heroism, however, masked a temptation that in the long run could destabilize a person if it turned inwards and became an end in itself.[117] Thus it was that certain dissidents, though they showed exemplary courage, were not always able to re-adapt themselves to normal life on their return from captivity.

After having played cat and mouse with a recalcitrant dissident for a while, the KGB would act: the delinquent would be arrested, indicted, interrogated again; subjected to new mental, and eventually physical, torture; judged, condemned and sent to the gulag. The fight against the dissidents was given to Andropov, who had become head of the KGB to erase the consequences of the de-Stalinization program. After the trial of Siniavsky and Daniel, there was a whole series of other political trials.[118][119] KGB agents tried to force the accused to make a confession and to show "sincere repentance", as in the good old days under Stalin, but they rarely succeeded. However, a new type of repression was tried: indefinite internment in "special" psychiatric hospitals where the "patients" were filled with hard neuroleptic drugs, along with heavy repeated doses of insulin.

All the same, the protest movement that began to show itself during the trial of Siniavsky and Daniel continued to grow. From that time on, the dissidents tried to make public every arrest, trial, and internment. Groups were formed for the purpose of defending human rights. In 1974, thanks to Solzhenitsyn , the Russian Social Fund was created to help political prisoners and their families. Two great figures marked this struggle: Solzhenitsyn and Sakharov.

Solzhenitsyn compared himself to a kneeling man who slowly, throughout his whole life, straightens up to his full stature; to a man who decided to abandon his self-enforced silence and to speak.[120] He was the first to dare to make a frontal attack on Soviet ideology and launched repeated appeals to fellow citizens not to participate in the big lie. During the growing intensity of his defiance of official power, Solzhenitsyn's work on the camps, *The Gulag Archipelago*, exploded like a bomb. In 1974 the authorities finally had him arrested, imprisoned, and forcibly exiled from the USSR.

Sakharov, on the other hand, belonged to that category of high-ranking Soviet scientists, the fair-haired boys of the regime, whose every need the government tried to satisfy. "One fine morning, he felt--or rather he had always felt it, since his birth--that all this abundance in which the government tried to drown him was nothing but dust and that his soul was looking for truth and justice."[121] Abandoning everything, Sakharov totally gave himself over to the struggle for human rights. He was present at all the political trials, staying outside of the courtroom when he was not allowed to enter. People of every background and from all over the country came to him for help.

Despite all its efforts, it took the KGB about fifteen years to beat down the dissidents. Besides repression, it utilized another means to weaken the opposition.

Beginning in 1970, under pressure from international opinion and after having launched a violent anti-Semitic campaign, the authorities allowed a certain number of Jews to emigrate to Israel each year. Soviets who were not in any way Jewish poured through the breach and had invitation certificates sent to them from Israel so that they could leave the Soviet Union. In order to get rid of certain dissidents, the KGB itself encouraged them to emigrate via Israel. A bargain was thus offered to them in these words: "If you don't go to the West, we will see that you go to the East." The East, of course, meant Siberia. The repression intensified especially after the invasion of Afghanistan in 1979 and the Moscow Olympic Games of 1980. It was then that Sakharov was sent to Gorky under house arrest. The repression reached its highest intensity after the death of Brezhnev in 1982, when Andropov took over the party. The reign of fear had begun again.

All through the period that followed Khrushchev's fall, the religious feeling of the people changed very noticeably. In a text circulated in the samizdat press at the beginning of the eighties, one observer made the following comment: "Ask a dozen of your friends who seem to be unbelievers if God exists. They will immediately answer, 'No, God does not exist.' Then, after a minute's reflection, nine out of ten will add, 'No, but there is of course something!'"

The author went on to say that this double reaction was not the result of a superstition or mental reservation "just in case", but rather a deep feeling that some kind of spiritual reality existed beyond the visible world. No one dared call that reality *God*, naturally. That word was as difficult for people to pronounce as it was to make their first sign of the cross. They had the impression that pronouncing the word *God*, in a context other than swearing or making fun, laid a very heavy responsibility on them. It was the first "yes" in a whole series of others, leading to many changes in their lives.

Those who admitted that "something" existed usually added, "Everyone has his own faith". Such faith was often comprised of spiritual principles and moral rules defining good and evil, and a number of rather vague religious ideas, including among others: the obligation of baptizing a child, of burying parents and loved ones from the church, and putting crosses on tombs.

After having given up on the paradise of a collectivized future, individuals turned in on themselves. They became especially concerned about their careers and personal comforts; under the circumstances, many were led to question the goal and meaning of their existence. The question was not always asked in an explicit way, but people's attitudes toward the faith, religion, and the Church manifested the presence of a deeper questioning. Scorn and ridicule gave way to curiosity, even to respect.[122]

In a letter to Pope Paul VI, written in 1967, Levitin wrote the following:

"Our young people are often a-religious, sometimes even peppered with antireligious prejudices; the result is that they consider religion to be a product of obscurantism and ignorance. However, they do not have the fanaticism and hatred of their grandfathers, and all the efforts of the professional religion-fighters during Khrushchev's time have completely failed to rekindle such feelings. In addition, our young people can take an interest in religion; they no longer refuse even to acknowledge its existence. They do not have their fathers' cold and scornful indifference. A typical Soviet young person has a feeling of mistrust mixed with curiosity toward religion." [123]

Soviet young people began to be seen wearing, not only jeans, but crosses as well--to the great displeasure of the Komsomol journal (the publication of the Communist youth movement); the paper never stopped warning young people against this latter practice, even though the Komsomol leaders explained it as a paradoxical indication of the progress of atheism:

"Everyone knows that religion is the opium of the people. In the mind of many young people, this statement is so obvious that its meaning has not penetrated into the depths of their consciousness. Is this not the reason why some young people "discover" religion, not as obscurantism, but as a pretty thing of the past, as attractive rites? And what is more, above a piece of modern furniture of varnished wood, we see a wall covered with icons. We also notice that certain people are wearing crosses, obviously as art objects, as a sign of being in fashion..."[124]

There was yet another external sign: "Communist" funerary monuments in the form of pyramids or obelisks with five-pointed stars on them fell out of use. In cemeteries, nearly all the tombs were once again decorated with crosses.

A new custom spontaneously appeared at the end of the seventies: people began to go en masse to the cemeteries on Easter Day to commemorate the dead. The phenomenon grew to such proportions that in Moscow the city had to organize a special bus service to accommodate the crowds.[125]

Families once again began, more or less, to celebrate Christmas and Easter. They did not go to church, obviously, but there were more and more people who knew that these days were important Orthodox feast days. The bakeries even sold *kulichi*, the traditional Easter cakes, but given the more "secular" name of "spring cakes".

In a certain segment of the population, there was a growing interest in yoga, parapsychology, paranormal phenomena, UFOs, astrology, and the occult; in other words, everything that was a substitute for religion. In short, an increasingly noticeable spiritual hunger made itself felt.

There were always grandmothers -*babushki*- to be seen in the churches, everyone always used to say. But not the same ones! The *babushki* of the seventies had been twenty years old at the time of the collectivization. Many had followed the general trend and had not found the road to the church until after their retirement.

It was obvious that religion was no longer the monopoly of uneducated old women. Young people, intellectuals, and men were turning to God.

According to the first objective Soviet study on the state of the faith, published by the authorities in 1987, the composition of those attending religious services had noticeably changed during the seventies, at least in Moscow and Leningrad, where it was less risky to go to church than in smaller towns. Though aged women continued to make up the majority, the number of men, especially among the young and those of mature years, had also greatly increased. Young people from eighteen to thirty formed a distinct group from now on.

Believers who had come to the faith without having received any religious education at home, and often against the wishes of their families, made up about one-third of the regular worshipers in the two largest cities.[126]

Vladimir Zielinsky was a member of this new generation of Christians; in a very beautiful testimony to its spiritual path, he had this to say:

> "Whenever new, unexpected faces show up in Orthodox churches of our large cities, we can be certain that these young people have not come just tagging along with their grandmothers. They have come of their own will, without anyone having pushed them... In the families of these new converts, atheism has been the fundamental principle since the 1930's. They come for their own reasons, reasons that have roots in the depths of their souls."[127]

More and more often in Moscow, children of Communists, and even of old *kagebisti*,[128] were asking to be baptized. Levitin also noted that people of Jewish origin frequently asked to be baptized. He was filled with amazement when he thought of these young men and women who, only a little while before, had not had the slightest idea what religion was and who, by their movement toward the Church, ordinarily provoked bitter family conflicts, leading in some cases to complete rupture. In most cases, however, their conversions were made spontaneously.[129]

For one such person, everything began with a reading of Dostoevsky; for another, it was Berdyaev; for yet another, the study of icons; for a fourth, it was yoga exercises. Tatiana Goricheva tells the following story: While doing yoga, she accidentally came across a book that proposed the Lord's Prayer as a formula to be repeated indefinitely. So she began to recite it in an automatic way, without any expression, as though it were a mantra, when suddenly she was completely bowled over: "It was not my stupid reason but my whole being that understood that He existed."[130]

A priest once related that, even up to the present, he was unable to explain his own conversion. Why, at the age of twenty, had he begun to go to church? Why had he dared to approach the priest after the liturgy and to ask him to be baptized? His whole family decided that he was overworked, that he had gone crazy, that he needed a "head doctor". He tried to find some explanation himself. Maybe he had found the faith because of the prayers of his great-grandmother. Maybe what happened to him was the result of his complete rejection of all official doctrine, along with its "sacred" authors. Maybe he had a too lively and too early passion for Dostoevsky and Soloviev. The priest concluded his search for a meaning to his conversion with these words:

> "If we look at things only from the outside, everything is born and dies in about the same way, but I am sure that no story that talks about a birth or death is anything like the inner experience of the person being born or dying. It I the same, I think, for the path that leads to God, for each baptism. The study of typology and sociology is one thing; the life of the soul is another. Why and how did I come to the faith? In the final analysis, I have no idea."[131]

Fr. Jacques Loew became a Christian as an adult, and his conversion took him all over the world: he lived with the worker priests of Marseilles and in the base communities of Brazil; he went to the School of Faith in Fribourg, Switzerland. When it was difficult to do so and required great caution, he went on several trips to the USSR in order to meet Christians. Fr. Jacques was also quite struck by the testimony of believers there: most of them had been, without any sign of warning, brusquely seized by God in the manner of an Andre Frossard or a Maurice Clavel:

"I met men and women from twenty to thirty-five years of age; they were lively, intelligent, cultivated; often scientists; neither especially well-off nor especially unhappy. They had grown up in an atmosphere in which there had not been the slightest whiff of religion. The name of Jesus was as foreign to them as the name of some god from India, but one fine day, they "caught God", as we might say that they "caught a cold", without knowing where, by whom, or how... They were people who, one day during a walk or a yoga session, suddenly became absolutely sure of the existence of God, not of some theory called "God", but of Someone."

"Their discovery of God is exactly like the call that Abraham heard: "Arise and go...", and Abraham got up and went. What a long path to travel. Where could they find a Christian to confide in, a priest they could ask for baptism without the authorities finding out--for the law said priests had to report the names of every newly-baptized person. Where could they find a Bible? This "wandering in the desert" often lasted for several years before they were actually baptized."[132]

To meet and talk with a priest, especially in smaller towns, was a risky business. What is more, priests, as a result of their background, education, and forced isolation from the mainstream society, were not generally well prepared for a meeting with these new believers who were separated from the tradition of the Church by a cultural abyss. As a result, rare were the priests who knew how to speak to these new converts, hungry as they were to hear a living word that spoke to their personal experience.

WITH FR. ZHELUDKOV

FR. SCHPILLER

FRS. VLADIMIR SMIRNOV
(LEFT) AND TAVION

In Moscow during the sixties, Fr. Vsevolod Schpiller was highly respected, especially among the intellectuals.[133] He was a former emigre who had returned to Russia after the Second World War, a man of culture and independent thinking. His Lenten sermons, especially, always drew large and attentive crowds to his parish, St. Nicholas of the Blacksmiths.

Fr. Dudko was a parish priest in an outlying neighborhood and during this time baptized many adults. His simple sermons, which also drew large numbers, were easily understood by all. He became particularly well known in 1973, when he began to have an informal question-and-answer session after Vespers each Saturday night. The authorities could not help but take notice and offense that "too many" people were coming to listen. After a year, they engineered Fr. Dudko's transfer to a parish far from Moscow.

All during this time, the parish of St. Elias, not far from the Kremlin, was a source of real spiritual support for many. The priests there, especially a Fr. Vladimir,[134] ministered in a discreet but effective way.

During their spiritual searching, certain young people found laymen capable of instructing them; these encounters took place in the framework of purely friendly, informal relations. Anatoli Levitin played this role with a fervor that his years in the gulag had not diminished, but he was once again arrested in 1969, and finally exiled after three years of prison camp. In a totally different manner, an old lady named Olga Nikolaevna,[135] whom people visited in her room in a community apartment in Moscow's old district, initiated more than one new convert to the life of the Church.

Even though he lived in Pskov, Fr. Zheludkov regularly went to Moscow. In 1968, he was touched by a letter of support written to a group of dissidents on trial. The following night, in a very strange fashion, he saw Pope John XXIII in a dream--the pope had been dead for five years. The good pope pointed to the dissidents, telling Fr. Zheludkov that they were fine people but that they had no priest among them. From that moment on, he got involved in the movement for human rights and was indeed a witness for the Church among the dissidents.[136]

In the smaller towns, the new Christians found certain monks and nuns who were known to be open and welcoming, such as the higumen of the Monastery of the Caves near Pskov,[137] or Fr. Tavrion[138] in Latvia. One of the great difficulties that the new believers had to deal with was isolation. They were not understood by their various communities and often had to hide their conversions. For the most part, they had no one in their day-to-day existence with whom they could share their faith. There existed hardly any kind of community life in the Church. The law expressly forbade parish associations to organize any kind of meeting, especially for prayer or Bible study, nor was there any opportunity for material aid, either. Nonetheless, some lay people took initiatives to try to deal with this need.

Being from Latvia but residing in Moscow, Sandr Riga had lived the fast life, but he too had been suddenly "seized". After his conversion, he felt the division between Christians as a terrible weight.

"We were friends. We wanted to walk together. We had just become converts and were filled with strength and optimism... Many people listened to us and found the path to God. They renounced drugs and alcohol... Many started to go to church. We became Orthodox, Catholic, or Protestant. Our conversion, our entry into the Church was a great joy, but there was always a question that tormented us when we got together: after having chosen a certain confession, would our paths from then on move apart?"[139]

Thus from about 1971, new converts from various confessions began to gather around Sandr Riga, a Catholic; they met together regularly in small groups in various people's apartments. They named their group Oecumena, but their group was less centered on ecumenical dialogue as practiced in the west than on common prayer, mutual help, and charitable work. Sandr Riga and his friends thus contributed to the development of community life among Christians.

Born in 1950 and the son of a communist, Alexander Ogorodnikov woke up to the faith after seeing Pasolini's film *The Gospel According to St. Matthew* at the Moscow Film Institute were he was studying, and from which he was soon expelled due to his beliefs. A nonconformist by nature, he was attracted to the hippie movement. Later, after being baptized in the Orthodox Church, he organized a group called the "Christian Seminar" for the study of the Russian religious renaissance.[140] The young converts in the group met regularly to deepen their religious education, but in addition they were moved by the desire to live in a "loving Christian community". The former members of this group bear witness today to the importance of this last aspect of the Seminar's inspiration for them.

Nevertheless, many temptations stalked the new converts. Some felt the need to affirm themselves and sometimes got caught up in an activism that they identified as authentic Christian life. Others took Christianity for an ideology; one which they hoped to substitute for Soviet ideology. Still others sought to escape from the Soviet reality, and made their faith a hiding place. Finally, yet another group confused aesthetic feelings, which the beauty of the liturgy had awakened, with spiritual life. Such confusions brought falls with them, sometimes shattering ones.

After Khrushchev's ouster, the massive frontal attacks against the Church stopped, though the persecution continued in more subtle and insidious ways. Administrative harassment became the favorite tactic. As a result, in 1965 the Council for the Affairs of the Orthodox Church was fused with another body, the Council for Religious Affairs, and this new bureau was given increased powers. At about the same time, the government decided to create municipal commissions to watch over the activities of priests and parishes. Many regulations were issued concerning "violations of the law on religious bodies".

According to a new constitution adopted in 1977, which made many references to Marxism-Leninism, atheism was implicitly raised to the status of a state religion. Believers continued to be thought of as second-class citizens and were the objects of all kinds of discrimination. If someone was known for his religious beliefs, he was denied access to numerous professions and had no chance of pursuing a career. While it was possible to go to religious services in Moscow or Leningrad without any great risk, this could not be done elsewhere with the same impunity. In other cities, there were in general no more than two functioning churches, and it was difficult to go there without being noticed, thus exposing oneself to all sorts of problems. For example, if a couple got married in church or if parents openly had their child baptized, they were quickly called on the carpet at work by a workers' committee whose job it was to re-educate them.

The guardians of ideological purity were especially anxious to keep children free of any religious influence. The Family Code of 1968 obliged parents to give their children a Communist education, necessarily atheistic. According to one Soviet jurist, "the

WITH FR. DUDKO AT
AN EXPOSITION IN
1975.

law does not forbid parents from giving religious instruction to their children, but what kind of education is it when certain parents teach their children the idea that everything that exists has a divine origin?"[141]

Finally, as in the past, there were very few religious books published: some liturgical books for the clergy, the monthly *Journal of the Moscow Patriarchate*, and from time to time, the Bible or the New Testament. But even these books were never found in bookstores, and since they were printed in such small quantities, the general population never even saw them.

Many letters and petitions drew attention to the repressions that believers had to undergo. This was especially done by Fr. Yakunin, who in 1976 created the Christian Committee for the Defense of Believers' Rights. In five years, through the samizdat press, more than four hundred documents were distributed in the USSR concerning violations of the freedom of religion.

In addition, voices were regularly raised to denounce the passivity of the hierarchy in the face of government action. In particular, a big stir was created by a letter from Solzhenitsyn to Patriarch Pimen[142], the successor of Alexei I, who had died in 1970.

Starting in 1979, the anti-religious policy was noticeably intensified. It seems that the authorities suddenly became aware of the depths of the religious awakening among young people and decided to react. What is more, to insure that the Moscow Olympic Games of 1980 went off smoothly, the government decided that it would be advisable to eliminate a certain number of "undesirable elements" from the capital. Finally, the invasion of Afghanistan in 1979 went hand in hand with a general hardening of attitudes.

Above all, it was necessary to intimidate and neutralize Christian activists. As a result, Fr. Yakunin, along with several other members of the Christian Committee for the Defense of Believer's Rights and several participants in Alexander Ogorodnikov's Seminar (he himself was already in Siberia), and Fr. Dudko were arrested. In June 1980, Christian circles got a very painful surprise: Fr. Dudko appeared on television and publicly repented of his past actions. His spiritual children were profoundly troubled. He had already gone through the trial of the gulag but had not stood up to several months of detention, to all the moral pressure put on him. The day after his televised confession, he was released. At the same time however, a whole series of trials was going on. Two accused persons pleaded guilty and got off with suspended sentences. Who was going to cast the first stone against them? They had overestimated their own strength, and it was they who had reproached Fr. Alexander, fifteen years previously, for being too timid. One of them even went so far as to tell him that they did not belong to the same Church. Others did not give in and were condemned to several years of detention camps and exile. In his final declaration, full of dignity and serenity, Fr. Yakunin thanked God for having allowed him to take part in the defense of believers' rights. Ogorodnikov was tried again but was fearless. He jumped up during one hearing, ran to a window and threw it wide open, and began to speak to his friends who were gathered outside. Both of these men continued their struggle in the gulag by engaging in a hunger strike to force the authorities to give them a Bible.

The years that followed Brezhnev's death saw an intensification of repression on all sides. For believers, there was no let up in the storm before 1987.

A Baptism in an Apartment

A Priest for a New
Generation of Believers

CHAPTER 7

THE CHURCH AT NOVAYA DEREVNIA

FR. ALEXANDER AND HIS FAMILY

When the abbey ceased to exist after his transfer to Tarasovka, Fr. Alexander carried out his pastoral duties for nearly twenty-five years without much change in the conditions of his ministry. In 1988 however, the Soviet authorities radically modified their religious policy. Up to that time, Fr. Alexander had fulfilled his mission with discretion, in the shadows, trying as much as possible to avoid an open confrontation with the government. He wanted to be available to the new generation of Russians who were beginning to free themselves from the illusions of Communist ideology and who were searching. He answered their questions and patiently led them to discover Jesus Christ. During the time of the abbey, he had at first not had many parishioners, but as time went on, the number of those coming to see him greatly increased. His fame spread by word of mouth. All these comings and goings got the pastor of the parish very worried; he kept a close eye on Fr. Alexander and finally sent a letter to the KGB denouncing his vicar's activities. Fr. Alexander wrote to Metropolitan Pimen of Krutitsy—later to become Patriarch— the administrator of the diocese of Moscow, asking to be transferred to another parish.[143] The metropolitan immediately granted his request, but the parishioners did not want to let him go. They signed petitions and caused such a commotion that Metropolitan Pimen was forced to send a telegram to the parish revoking his decision! Fr. Alexander's popularity with the parishioners won him the "privilege" of serving for yet another year with this informer. Having to serve at the altar with this man was particularly painful. One day however, the pastor of a neighboring parish some six miles north of Tarasovka, offered to exchange vicars with Fr. Alexander's superior. This sick and aging priest wanted to have a young and dynamic assistant. The transfer took place during the summer of 1970. This time Fr. Alexander left Tarasovka in near secrecy, but as incredible as it may seem, his former rector was very sad to see him leave!

Fr. Alexander served the parish of Novaya Derevnia until his death in 1990; he was vicar until 1989, when he was named rector.

When he left Alabino, Fr. Alexander had needed to find lodging at Tarasovka, and later, in Novaya Derevnia as well, as the parish did not have a special house for the priest. This he found in Semkhoz, the little village where he lived until his death, in an izba situated in the middle of a garden. He was very much attached to this little wooden house. His door was always open for his friends, his parishioners, and even strangers who had come a long way to meet him. Dostoevsky once wrote that every man should know that somewhere, someone is waiting for him. Semkhoz was just such a place, where everyone who came, felt that he had been expected.[144]

One of Fr. Alexander's friends once confided, "If anyone were to ask me what heaven must feel like, I would answer, 'exactly like being at Fr. Alexander's house'. There was nothing really spectacular there, but it felt so good, like no other place: full of freedom, light, and warmth, free of anything superfluous. The harmony instilled by the master of the house emanates from every object in it."[145] Just as on a plane, people could be completely at ease while being unconscious of the altitude.

Nonetheless, Fr. Alexander more often received guests at his parish. Semkhoz is, after all, more than ninety minutes from Moscow. The house is not very easy to find, and besides, Fr. Alexander enjoyed a certain amount of tranquility there, no doubt necessary for his equilibrium. After an exhausting day, he liked to go home to be alone, not with himself but in quiet intimacy with God. It was there that he wrote, and he often used to say that, had he lived in Moscow, he would never have been able to write his books.

Everything in his house was simple and impeccably kept, a situation quite different from so many Russian homes. ("We seem to be camped out in our homes", wrote a Russian thinker at the beginning of the last century.) For this writer, it was obvious that the attention accorded even to small things was part of the creative work that was the duty of each Christian.

In 1988, Fr. Alexander had the joy of enlarging his house, thus having a bit more space; he naturally had to deal with all the problems inherent in this kind of work in a Communist land.

Fr. Alexander's wife was an accountant, and he did not disdain to help with the housework , often doing the shopping. He took over all the laborious domestic tasks and also tended the vegetable garden. He felt that in the life of today's couples, there are no tasks that belong solely to the wife; he also knew how to cook. When his wife was out, but he had visitors, he himself would prepare the meals: laughing, humming, and reciting poetry, sometimes in Greek or Hebrew.

The parish of Novaya Derevnia, where Fr. Alexander served for exactly twenty years, is dedicated to the feast of the Presentation in the Temple.[146]   In Russia the feast is called "the Meeting". The meeting which gives the feast its name occurs between the child Jesus and the Old Testament. Christ has come to bring light to the nations, that is, to unbelievers. When the Virgin Mary presented her Son to Simeon, the old man told her that her soul would be pierced by a sword. Does not this dedication to the Meeting of Christ in the Temple symbolize Fr. Alexander's whole ministry?

His parish church was a wooden building, no doubt one of the simplest and most modest churches around Moscow. Curiously enough, it had been built in another village after the Revolution, then dismantled, and put up again in Novaya Derevnia after the Second World War.

The village is situated on both sides of the old road that runs from Moscow to Zagorsk; it is therefore long and narrow. At one time, several hundred yards away, a parallel route was constructed, thus avoiding the populated area. At the end of the sixties, this road was improved with the Moscow Olympics of 1980 in mind. This was the road foreign tourists were to take to visit Zagorsk, and beyond that, Rostov and Yaroslavl, where they could see the jewels of ancient Russian architecture. One day, a commission which was participating in preparation for the Games passed by, and realized that the honorable visitors going to Zagorsk might see the little church, the miserable condition of which would make a very bad impression. So they enlarged the church by adding on a new, more spacious narthex (i.e., a vestibule). The commissioners also renovated the small bell tower and porch, and not in bad taste, either.

The closest train station was a few kilometers away at Pushkino.

As with many country churches, the parish of Novaya Derevnia was mostly frequented by old women. When Fr. Alexander arrived, however, new people started to come, mainly on Sundays and feast days; these included other faithful- intellectuals, young people, and visitors from Moscow. The two groups did not always get along. The newcomers did not always know how to behave in an Orthodox church or how to make the sign of the cross. Some of them crossed their arms during the service - this was simply not done!; young girls came into the church with their heads uncovered and - horror of horrors!- wearing pants. There were, of course,, some *babushki* who tried to teach them what to do. At the beginning, the young people for the most part scorned these uneducated women, not understanding the way they expressed their faith. With patience and goodness, and with his own skill as well, Fr. Alexander succeeded in getting the two groups to accept each other, along with their differences.

Fr. Alexander is often presented as the priest for intellectuals, but he never neglected the simple people who were his parishioners from the village and the surrounding area. They respected him and believed in the force of his prayer. He went into nearly everyone's home, visiting nearly every family to give communion to the sick, to anoint the sick and dying, to bless an apartment. Everyone could feel his warmth and ability to communicate.[147]

Next to the church, there was a little wooden house where the priests, choir members, and servers could get ready for a service or have a meal, and where the priests could stay overnight when, at certain times of the year, the length and number of services kept them from going home. In this house, Fr. Alexander had a very small office with a couch to sleep on. It was there that people usually found him. If that little office could only talk! How many men and women, who no longer believed in anything, found meaning for their lives in that office? How many, who had lost all hope, left with new strength? How many, by telling the long story of their past, made their first confession in that little house? How many were secretly baptized there? How many made their first sign of the cross there, tracing the form with a stiff and heavy gesture as though being held back by some physical force?

How many of his spiritual children are unable to forget their first meeting with Fr. Alexander? The following story is typical of so many. Someone once told a friend about a certain priest and explained how to get to his church. Then one day, at Moscow's Yaroslavl Station, the friend got on the train to Zagorsk. Getting off at Pushkino and taking the bus to the big highway, he followed the lower, parallel road past the izbas until he saw the little blue cupola in the middle of the trees. He entered the church but stayed at the back, afraid, lowering his head when the parishioners made the sign of the cross. Maybe Fr. Alexander nodded to the visitor when he saw the unfamiliar face as he went in front of the iconostasis to say certain prayers, or when he circled the inside of the church to cense the icons. Then after the service, in the courtyard, the visitor went up to the priest and was asked to wait. The wait was long, very long, somewhat worrisome. The friend had certainly never met a priest. Could he really confide in such a man? Finally, both men went into the little house and its office, and there, right from the first words, the newcomer lost all apprehension and mistrust. He had before him a friend who listened to every word; the man felt loved immediately. Many people dealt with Fr. Alexander, but with him, everyone had the feeling of having struck up a unique and special friendship. Even if the meeting was a brief one, even if many people were present, each person always had a moment of true communication, heart to heart. All Fr. Alexander's attention was exclusively turned toward the person to whom he was speaking. Fr. Alexander saw someone special in each person, whom he loved with a special love.

Following this first meeting, the friend returned more than once to Novaya Derevnia, maybe humming some verses of the poet

Galich, whom Fr. Alexander had baptized. Galich had left Russia at the beginning of the sixties, but was never able to adapt to life as an emigre. He wrote a nostalgic song called *The Day I Return*, and some of the lines speak about the little church of Novaya Derevnia:

> The day I return
> I will go into that special house
> Where the sky is no rival to the blue cupola,
> Where the smell of incense, like the smell of bread given out at the soup kitchen,
> Will suddenly grab me, dazzling my heart.
> The day I return...
> Oh, the day I return!

Then, as on the first day, the newcomer walked the one hundred steps to the courtyard, or else he entered the house, going into the main room, which was used as a dining room. There, those who were already crowded around the table waiting for their turn, chattering away, moved apart to make room for him. Each time his patience was rewarded; each time he received the same welcome.

Fr. Alexander was not satisfied just to receive these new or future believers at Novaya Derevnia. He frequently went to see them in Moscow. With those who could not take the risk of being seen at Novaya Derevnia, he made an appointment for a meeting in a friend's apartment. He also often baptized adults and children at their apartments.

At that time, people who were baptized or had their children baptized in a church inevitably attracted attention and exposed themselves to serious problems, but a priest who performed baptisms secretly also ran heavy risks. In fact, in order to serve in a parish, a priest had to have, not only the approval of his bishop, but also the proper registration with the city government. Therefore, any cleric caught baptizing without having it noted in the parish register could have his registration taken away by the local city officials.

For Fr. Alexander, these friendly meetings with newcomers provided occasions to pursue his conversations with men and women who were searching for meaning in their lives; at the same time, he could give them catechesis in an informal way. We must not forget that in the Soviet Union, unlike the West, there was no place where Christians could gather together except at the liturgy. Such meetings were, in fact, expressly forbidden by law.

It is not hard to see how these meetings somewhat resembled those of the early Christians. Such gatherings were, of course, far from the ideal described in the Acts of the Apostles; nonetheless, they represented the rudiments of community life.

Fr. Alexander described his outlook in the following way:

> "When I became a priest, I tried to unite the parish, to make it one community and not just a group of people who knew very little about each other, whom fortune had thrown together. I wanted all the members to help one another, to pray together, to study the Scriptures together, and to receive communion together."[148]

To those who spoke to him, Fr. Alexander gave spiritual, moral, and material support. Once he had baptized people, he then regularly heard their confessions, gave them communion and baptized their children; he blessed their new apartments after they had moved in. He advised them on how to develop good marital, familial, and professional relations. He helped them with their intellectual work and found them a doctor; he pointed out people who could provide various needed services. On occasion, he also helped people in financial need by discreetly slipping some rubles between the pages of a book on a table. He often took out little gifts from his big bulging briefcase: precisely the thing that someone needed and that he had been able to find. This was again a sign of the attention he paid to each person.

In the summertime, many of his friends often rented summer homes around Novaya Derevnia. Russians love nature very much, and when the weather gets pleasant, Muscovites can think of only one thing: to get out of the capital and to go live in a summer home, or *dacha*, as it is called. These summer residences are simple wooden homes- izbas-, whose owners rent out one or several rooms to city dwellers during the summer months. Even though these places are not very comfortable, they are not far from the forest; children, usually watched over by a grandmother, can thus play out in the open while the parents come and visit on the weekends. Novaya Derevnia is a fairly civilized place and is close enough to Moscow so that people can live there and still go to work in the heart of the capital. Fr. Alexander's mother also rented a room and a veranda in a house close to the church, belonging to an old lady in the village. Many people came to see her, especially after Sunday liturgy. Thus, the little community could grow even closer together during the summer.

At first, it was an informal group of friends of the kind so well loved in Russia. Fr. Alexander relied on this group, and especially on his mother, to welcome new converts. He was very concerned that the newcomers not be abandoned to their own devices; with their new but still fragile faith, they had to live out their beliefs in the hostile environment of Soviet society. At that period, these new Christians could not easily confide in their friends, even the most intimate ones, who would simply not have been able to understand. Young adults from twenty to twenty-five often hid their conversions even from their parents.

At the end of the sixties, however, this rather informal circle could no longer meet the needs of the increasing number of people coming to the faith through Fr. Alexander's work. He then set up little groups that got together regularly, normally once a week.[149] These groups were all centered on common prayer and mutual help; they had, at the same time, different specific tasks. Some groups were specially given over to the catechesis of new members, whom they prepared for baptism or whom had already come to be baptized. Others concentrated on the study of the Bible. Still others interested themselves in theological questions or Church history, learning from those books which could be found: works published before the Revolution, books in Russian printed abroad and acquired clandestinely, as well as books in foreign languages, which required translation. The groups met in the apartment of one of the members of the group. Some always met in the same place. Others gathered more cautiously, sometimes at one, sometimes at another, place; so as not to attract the attention of nosy neighbors who would have been more than happy to denounce the groups.

These groups participated in the same liturgical and sacramental life of the parish church of the Presentation at Novaya Derevnia. Not everyone could come each Sunday because of the distance or the danger of being noticed. Fr. Alexander nonetheless insisted that they come regularly. They took part in the great feasts, especially Pascha[150], the feast of feasts of the Orthodox Church, with a very special fervor.

Thus there was built up a form of parish life particularly adapted to the conditions specific to the Soviet Union, where only the celebration of the liturgy was authorized, all other activity being forbidden to believers and having to take place in secret.

Fr. Alexander's groups, though independent of any movement in the West, paralleled the attempts among Western Christians of the same period to find the meaning of ecclesial communion on the basis of small groups.[151]

Fr. Alexander insisted on the significance of the sacraments and the necessity of preparing for them. To adults who came to him for baptism, he often said, "Wait; take your time; read and re-read the Gospel; let it soak in! I will know when you are really ready, and then I will set the date myself."[152]

He once wrote,

"It is a good thing that adults ask to be baptized, but it is still too soon for rejoicing. Let's not forget the Lord's words: 'Whoever believes and is baptized will be saved'.[153] Don't forget that Christ first speaks about believing. In baptism, the new Christian not only receives the gift of grace, but he also promises before God to live according to His will."[154]

As for little children, it was the parents who made the promise in their name. Unfortunately, often the parents who wanted to have their children baptized barely knew how to make the sign of the cross themselves, but priests never sent them away. "Children need grace, and the parents' simple desire, confused and unconscious, to tie them to the Church takes the place of faith in the Lord's eyes. The only thing left for us to do is to pray that God Himself will instruct these children."[155]

Baptism is a decisive stage in the spiritual struggle that sometimes manifests itself in outward and visible signs. One of Fr.

Alexander's friends mentioned the doubts that suddenly over-took him on the eve of his baptism. He asked himself:

> "What are you doing? To wear a cross around your neck, kiss icons, light candles with old women, fast... Really! How could I have come to this: to voluntarily throw myself into the arms of a Church of yes-men that approves everything the State does? No, Fr. Alexander is an exception, and I, like everyone else who has not conformed to the party line, I am looking for consolation. Does this eternal life really exist, this Kingdom of Heaven?"

So it was decided. The friend would not go to Novaya Derevnia. He went to bed but did not fall asleep; then he was suddenly gripped by a bout of dizziness. At that moment he saw the icon on the wall of his room and made the sign of the cross. All of a sudden, he recovered his serenity. The next day Fr. Alexander baptized him as planned, and the friend told him about what he had experienced some hours before. Fr. Alexander apologized for not having warned him. This experience was quite common; a typical attack of the forces of evil. It would happen that people who were coming to be baptized fell asleep on the train, and woke up after having gone by the station; sometimes they got on the wrong train and found themselves in some strange place.[156]

Fr. Alexander took great care to teach the faith to those who wanted to be baptized and carefully guided them toward the proper disposition of heart and mind. In particular, he prepared them through a long confession. A woman of his parish recalled her surprise when he invited her to sit down in front of him in a chair, and to confide in him as though he were an intimate, long-time friend. She thus began to tell him her life story, lasting through several sessions.[157] Another parishioner told how, during his first confession, Fr. Alexander explained the importance of the Christian vocation, of the responsibility of becoming Christ's representatives. For Fr. Alexander, baptism was never just a simple ceremony; he truly baptized his people into Christ, the Son of God become man.[158]

He recommended that the members of his groups go to confession and communion at least once a month. In the Orthodox Church, as in the Catholic Church, the faithful up to rather recent times customarily went to communion only once a year, or when in danger of death. This practice, unknown to the early Church, was born out of a sense of our unworthiness and sin before the face of the grandeur of the eucharistic mystery. True, there had been men of the Church, such as Saint Seraphim of Sarov in eighteenth-century Russia, who recommended frequent communion. After the Revolution as well, some priests and small lay communities rediscovered frequent communion to be a vital necessity in the heat of persecution. The general practice, however, had not been modified. Fr. Alexander was one of those today within the Orthodox Church who advocated a general change in practice and a return to frequent communion.

In order to prepare the faithful to receive the body and blood of Christ, the Orthodox Church has maintained a strict eucharistic fast (no food or drink from the night before) and recommends that people attend Vespers the preceding evening, or Vigil on Saturday night if they intend to go to communion on Sunday. Orthodoxy closely ties the eucharist and confession: people must confess on the same day or the evening before going to communion. In general, priests hear confessions before the liturgy and ordinarily have to continue hearing them during most of the liturgy, sometimes even up to the very moment of communion. One priest hears confessions to the side of the iconostasis while the main celebrant serves at the central altar. When there are very many people, the priest proceeds with a general confession. These confessions can have a somewhat mechanical character: the priest enumerates a list of sins and the faithful mentally repent of those they have committed. Or, at the mention of this or that sin, they exclaim in a loud voice: 'Father, I have sinned'. Then each one approaches the priest, one by one, to receive absolution.

Fr. Alexander did not content himself with repeating a catalogue of sins, and always gave a sermon to help the faithful make an examination of conscience. During these confessions, he manifested his talent as a preacher, his experience of the spiritual life, and his feeling for his fellows. Many had the impression that he was speaking to them personally, to each one individually. As they came forward for the absolution, each had the opportunity for a brief exchange with him. It was St. John of Kronstadt who had inaugurated these penitential sermons. Other priests after the Revolution had followed his example. One in particular was Fr. Golubtsov, who was Fr. Alexander's spiritual father. During Khrushchev's persecutions, Fr. Golubtsov preached very little; it was then practically impossible to do so. He had been celebrated, however, for the penitential services he conducted.[159]

Nonetheless, Fr. Alexander felt that the faithful should not limit themselves merely to general confessions, but insisted that they needed to be alternated with private confessions, which permitted a genuine personal exchange with the priest. The importance Fr. Alexander gave to confession was determined both by his conception of his priestly ministry and by the context in which he exercised it.

The Soviet system was as destructive of souls as it had been in other domains. People sometimes speak of an anthropological catastrophe, a catastrophe that affected people's minds and hearts as much as Chernobyl affected their bodies. The participation in deceit which the regime required of all its subjects as a test of absolute obedience, was experienced as a secret humiliation, a deep wound inflicted on each person. Stalin had called upon to become "engineers of men's souls" as though the human personality could be built in the same way as a car. And so, in order to repair the disaster, doctors of the human soul were necessary. As Fr. Alexander recalled, the Church rightly compares a confessor to a doctor. Fr. Alexander was himself such a doctor par excellence, a patient physician who listened to people, comforted them, and put them at ease.

He cared for people out of the abundance of his love. No doubt, he heard people's confessions keeping in mind the words of the prophet Hosea, which Christ repeated on two different occasions: "It is love that I require, and not sacrifice".[160]

Fr. Alexander made clear the nature of the relation between the faithful and their spiritual father, that is, the priest to whom they regularly confess:

> "They should make no important decision without asking his blessing, or at least asking his advice. They should follow his guidelines about prayer, the frequency of communion, fasting, and service to others. By following his guidance, they also align their lives with what the Church asks."[161]

Unfortunately today in Russia, certain priests have transformed spiritual direction into a veritable tyranny; they have little experience, are themselves recent converts, and want to imitate the great spiritual fathers, the startsy of the past. Fr. Alexander always warned against this danger. He reminded people that a parish priest could not give the same kind of spiritual direction as a starets:

"We often think that the relation of spiritual child to spiritual father requires that the former always be obedient to the latter. In reality, this principle is an essential part of the monastic life. A monk promises to be obedient, to do whatever his spiritual father requires. A parish priest cannot impose such a model on lay people and cannot arrogate to himself the right to give peremptory orders. He must be happy recalling the Church's rules, orienting his parishioners' lives, and helping them in their inner struggles."[162]

The parish priest must keep himself from both paternalism and authoritarianism.

Fr. Alexander wanted to lead each person to the point of deciding for himself; he did not want to order or to impose. He compared his role to that of a midwife who is present only to help the mother give birth herself to her baby. One of his friends wrote that Fr. Alexander was "above us and yet right beside us".[163]

Even though he was a man bubbling over with activity, Fr. Alexander never stopped reminding people that prayer was indispensable to Christian life, that faith was nourished by prayer. He composed a little booklet, *A Practical Guide to Prayer*, in typewritten form, that he gave to his spiritual children to read.[164] In particular, he recommended that they not allow themselves to be discouraged by the difficulty that comes with trying to pray. It is a question of patience. A psychiatrist, who became his friend, told about a dialogue that he had with Fr. Alexander the day they met:

> *Fr. Alexander:* People no doubt ask you about things other than their illnesses. They must ask you questions, for example, about the meaning of life?

Psychiatrist: I too ask myself questions, especially on the meaning of death.

Fr. Alexander: Well, we too are searching. It is true that we have an "information   window", but we must be patient. We call that prayer...[165]

In ancient mythology, he used to say, there existed a person named Theia, who recovered his strength by touching the earth. We, on the contrary, renew our strength by touching heaven for an instant. All his friends bore witness to the intensity of his prayer.

Someone should gather up all the statements of those who claim to have been healed through his prayers. For example, one of his friends was dying in a resuscitation room of a cancer clinic. This friend told how he regained consciousness when he heard the voice of Fr. Alexander, who had come to visit him.

Everyone who ever met him was struck by his availability. He never refused to meet anyone even though people often came without any announcement. He would then leave everything to listen to whatever the person had to say, as if he had nothing else to do.

How did he manage to do it all: the parish ministry; all the people he received at his home and at Novaya Derevnia; all those he went to see in Moscow; the responsibility for the groups; catechesis; domestic chores; the triangular commutes between home, parish, and Moscow? And still he found time to keep abreast of cultural events, to pursue theological work, and to write articles and books.

He was no doubt blessed with an extraordinary capacity for work, a powerful memory, and a rare ability to concentrate. From child-

MARIA TEPNINA, A FORMER SPIRITUAL DAUGHTER OF FR. SERAPHIM WHO WAS WITH FR.
ALEXANDER FROM HIS BIRTH TO HIS DEATH, BETWEEN FR. ALEXANDER AND HIS BROTHER PAUL.

AT THE HOME OF
SOME FRIENDS.

FR. ALEXANDER GIVING COMMUNION, (RIGHT) ANDREI ERIOMIN

hood, he had learned not to waste time. As soon as he found a seat on the train, he took a sort of clipboard out of his briefcase; put a paper on it; and began to write.

Among his spiritual children, he naturally had people who were devoted to him, and on whom he could rely to carry out various tasks. When he had to go from Novaya Derevnia to Moscow, he was happy to make the trip by car with one or another of these close friends. The car then had the look of the field headquarters of a military chief of staff out on maneuvers!

Fr. Alexander knew how to use each minute of freedom. He always said:

> "When you work, work. When you pray, pray. When you play, play. Do nothing, however, in just any old way, in a mediocre manner. Don't remain idle, with nothing to do. Be very careful not to 'kill' time, for by 'killing' time, you are killing your own life."[166]

A priest who knew him once exclaimed, "I too am a priest; I am overwhelmed with work from morning to night, and each time I see a new book by Fr. Alexander, I always wonder: when and how does he find the time to do all that?" Fr. Alexander answered with a smile, looking to the icon corner: "Well, we have a contract. I give all I have; I give all my time, and in relation to my strength, I am able to succeed in what I have to do."[167]

Fr. Alexander's influence cannot, of course, be measured in numbers, but if necessary, the following statistics can be cited: in the seventies, there were several dozen of his small groups, each one often having several dozen people associated with it. On the average, Fr. Alexander performed about sixty baptisms a month, usually of adults.

Due to his open-mindedness, his encyclopedic knowledge, his taste for literature and the arts, and his interest in science, he was the ideal person to talk to intellectuals; he never responded to their queries with pat answers. How many well-known personalities - scientists, writers, artists - were evangelized by him? Today, when the precautions of previous years are no longer necessary, we are beginning to discover all the names with amazement.

One day at a painting exhibition—it must have been around 1966, when he was still at Tarasovka—a woman dressed in black came up to him and said, "It seems that you are very good at converting people. Well, I have some I need to convert." It was the pianist Maria Yudina, at the time quite famous in Russia. They became good friends, and later on used to have unending conversations while they walked around the Tarasovka church for hours on end.

During the same period, Fr. Alexander met Solzhenitsyn. Having read one of his books, distributed in samizdat, he wanted to meet the famous writer. A friend of Fr. Dudko arranged the meeting, which was cloaked in mystery, as the writer often had to hide in order to complete certain of his works. Three men arrived. Someone asked from the inside: "Who is there?" "Just the right person, just the right person," answered the friend, who didn't dare reveal any names. They were let into the house and looked each other over. From pictures, Fr. Alexander thought he would see a dark and ferocious figure, but instead he saw a strong man enter the room: joyful, laughing with a hearty laugh. He radiated a spiritual energy. "I have met a certain number of writers, but none had his intelligence. He understood very quickly, had a childlike enthusiasm, and made all sorts of plans." Following this first meeting, the two men met regularly. Solzhenitsyn had been baptized in his infancy, but was only beginning to

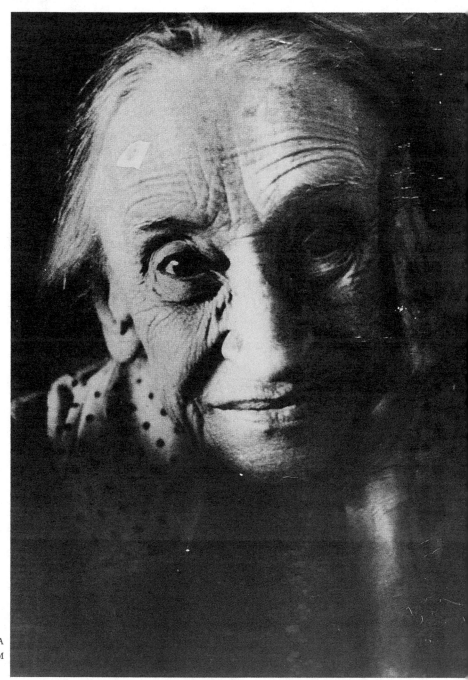

NADEZHDA
MANDELSTAM

awaken to the faith, and viewed Christianity as a sort of ethical system. He read certain of Fr. Alexander's books that, like his own, had not yet been published.[168]

Fr. Alexander was equally close to Nadezhda Mandelstam, the widow of the great poet[169][170] who had died in the gulag.[171] She also came to communion regularly at Novaya Derevnia. He visited her in Moscow and gave her the last sacraments on the eve of her death.

Fr. Alexander gloried in none of this. He was not in the least turned in on himself. He always remained extremely humble, and loved to present himself as a simple country priest. He once wrote the following in a letter:

"If people say that a writer is unique, it is a triumph. If they say that about a priest, it is a catastrophe. We are only simple

A. SOLZHENITSYN

soldiers. We live by our oath. We are among those who 'are not warriors if they go into battle alone.' It is true that we are protected from self-centeredness by our failures, the weight of responsibilities, fatigue, and danger. I also have a scientific mind, and science teaches modesty. I have done this or that, written one more book. So what? What is all that in comparison with the immensity of the task?"[172]

"That Which I Believe"

CHAPTER 8

On the eve of his death, Fr. Alexander gave a lecture on Christianity. He concluded in this way:

"If we ask ourselves once again what the essence of Christianity is, we must give the following answer: it is God-manhood; that is, the union of the human spirit, which is finite and limited in time, with the divine, which is infinite. It is the sanctification of the flesh from the moment the Son of Man adopted our joys and our sufferings: that which we construct, our love, our work, nature, the world in which He found Himself and in which He was born as man and as God-Man. None of that is rejected; nothing is humiliated. It is rather raised to a new level. In Christianity the world is sanctified: evil, darkness, and sin are vanquished. This is God's victory. This victory began on the night of the Resurrection, and it will continue as long as the world exists. I will stop here for today, and the next time...."[173]

These were Fr. Alexander's last public words. All his teaching was centered on Jesus Christ. One of his spiritual children related:

"Fr. Alexander could speak indefinitely about Jesus Christ, as though He were a close friend or relative, finding new traits in Him each time. In our time, when everything seems already to have been said, he was able to find new and effective words that could warm people's hearts."[174]

Christianity, he used to say, is not first and foremost a set of dogmas and moral precepts, but is above all Jesus Christ Himself.[175] "Mark well", he stressed in the course of the above lecture:

"Christ did not leave us a single written line, as Plato left the dialogues. And He did not leave us table with a law, as did Moses. Nor did He dictate the Koran, as did Mohammed. He did not found a religious order, like the Buddha. Rather He said: 'I am with you even till the end of time...' It is in this that the most profound experience of Christianity consists."[176]

Thus, the whole of Christian life is based on a personal, spiritual experience, on a personal meeting with Jesus Christ. A meeting.

That day, Fr. Alexander had explained the meaning of a prayer widely used in the Orthodox Church, a prayer based on the repetition of a simple formula, easy to repeat but difficult to master: "Lord Jesus Christ, have mercy on me a sinner".

"In repeating certain prayers, the Christian masters of prayer might be compared to those of the Orient, of India, who repeat various mantras. There is a similarity and a parallel, but one of the main prayers of Christian ascetics is called the Jesus prayer, and those who pray it constantly repeat the name of Him who was born, lived on earth, was crucified and rose from the dead. The Christocentrism of this important Christian prayer is what distinguishes it from all other forms of meditation and from all mantras; for it produces a meeting, not just a concentration of thought; not simply a plunge into some sort of ocean or abyss of spirituality, but rather a meeting between a person and Jesus Christ, who is above the world and in the world."[177]

In this lecture, Fr. Alexander used the expression 'God-manhood', unusual at least to our ears. This word was introduced by the Russian theologian Vladimir Soloviev, who had a great influence on Fr. Alexander. In fact, this new word sums up the single, foundational dogma of Christianity, the union of God with His creature:

> "This unique and unchangeable truth...has become an event thanks to the coming in the flesh of the true God-Man Jesus Christ, the personal center of the universal God-man-hood. The truth of the God-Man, who has already come in the flesh and who will come again in His glory, contains in itself all the fullness of the New Testament revelation."[178]

Fr. Alexander insisted on the necessary cooperation between man and God which is assumed by this union, this Covenant:

> "It is here that we have a basic difference with yoga, which believes that man can reach God, bring himself into His presence, by his own will. Christianity says to man: 'You can indeed make yourself better, but it is impossible to reach God before He has come to you.'"[179]

At the same time, grace does not act without man. It does not act as though someone waved a magic wand. It is not like some science-fiction novel in which a mysterious gas spreads over the earth and makes everyone good. This union requires man's total activity and commitment. The Gospel makes us participate in the process of divine creation. It makes us *co*-creators, *co*-participants, *co*-responsible.

Fr. Alexander recalled the reflection of a French positivist philosopher of the last century, who one day happened to enter a church. Soothed by the organ music, he experienced a sense of well-being. He felt himself to be in an unmoving ship. While everything went by, the ship, with its celestial organ music, remained still. All his problems, all the problems of the world, appeared insignificant to him. He just had to let himself be carried away by the music.

Fr. Alexander then cried out:

"this is not Christianity - this is the opium of the people! For those Christians who might be tempted to turn their faith into an easy chair, a refuge, a tranquil harbor, Marx's formula is a warning! No, Christianity is not a security blanket! We take risks in becoming Christians; it is not an insurance policy against a bad conscience.

"Authentic Christianity is, if you wish, a mountain climbing expedition, a dangerous and difficult undertaking. This is why there are so often substitutes to take its place. People stay at the bottom of the mountain. They close themselves up in their tent and read the guidebook, imagining that they are already on top. This same thing happens to us when we read the books of the mystics; we repeat their words and imagine ourselves to have arrived at the summit." [180]

Fr. Alexander regularly returned to the subject of the ambiguous relation that Christians have with the world:

"When we read in 1 John: 'Do not love the world or the things in the world'[181], this refers to the reign of sin. Yet in the Gospel also written by St. John, we read: 'God so loved the world that He gave His only-begotten Son.'[182] The New

Testament is ascetical in the sense that it teaches us to forget ourselves, so that we learn to struggle against sin; to purify our thoughts, our feelings, our acts; but it does not turn us away from earthly life. And yet, with time there appeared Christians of Manichaean inspiration, hating everything earthly and more resembling self-torturing Brahmins than disciples of Christ."[183]

"Take", said Fr. Alexander:

"the example of Saint Francis of Assisi, who left everything and became a vagabond, a beggar. At a certain level, he rejected the world; but at a higher level, he adopted it like another person. He loved nature, people, animals, grass, water, as no pagan was ever able to do: 'My sister the moon, my brother the sun.' This is something completely different than the gods of Antiquity. He accomplished a certain 'dialectical turn-around': having left the world so as to return and sanctify it by his love and his faith."

Fr. Alexander taught those who listened to him to discover the presence of God in the world. Every beautiful and good thing in men and every good thing they do comes from God, even if they do not know it, for man has been made in the image and likeness of the Creator. We must learn to recognize the hidden action of grace in the world, he used to say. We must not ever push goodness away, even when it comes from unbelievers. On the contrary, we should rejoice and consider it our own.

Fr. Alexander did not want his spiritual children to cut themselves off from life because they had converted, to kill their aspirations or to lose interest in their professional and social activities; this was a frequent temptation. On the contrary, faith should sanctify everything positive in their existence.

Being a Christian in the world today was for Fr. Alexander a complete program. If we were supposed to act like men of the nineteenth century, he often said laughingly, God would have put us in the nineteenth century! He insisted on this point for two reasons. On the one hand, asceticism occupies a privileged place in eastern Christianity. Yet, poorly understood, it can degenerate into scorn for the world and a global rejection of culture. This tendency is illustrated in Dostoevsky's novel *The Brothers Karamazov* by the behavior of the monk Therapont, who spent his life fasting and covered in chains. Fr. Therapont opposed Fr. Zossima, representing the Optina tradition with its spirit of openness. The intransigent ascetic had such a hatred for the gentle Zossima that he did not even hesitate to make a scene in front of his tomb after his death. On the other hand, new converts could not only believe that asceticism was the sole path of holiness, but they also found it hard to find their place in Soviet society. Since they often had to hide their faith even from their friends and family, they risked becoming "interior emigres", feeling like complete strangers in their own social and professional milieus. Fr. Alexander recommended that when we get together with our friends, Christians like ourselves, we should not imagine ourselves to be under a bell jar. In the Church, we should not forget that we are people of our time, living in the world.

On the outside, for example in our relations at work, it is not necessary to announce in a provocative manner that we are Christians, to cross ourselves demonstratively in public; we must, however, feel ourselves to be members of the Church and not forget for a minute that we are witnesses. It is necessary that people understand that we are not at all like everybody else-well and good! Thus on the day they learn that we belong to the Church, it will be to the Church's honor and not the reverse.

Fr. Alexander wrote the following in a letter:

"I don't understand very well the distinction drawn between the profane and the religious. For me, these words are pedestrian to the highest degree. Even though in my youth, people explained to me that there existed certain 'special subjects', this was due rather to the fact that we lived among people for whom all such talk was quite foreign. Little by little, this distinction has almost completely lost its meaning for me, because everything has become, in its own way, 'special'. Every aspect of life, every problem, everything that touches us seems to me directly linked to the Most High.

"To live as if 'religion' were an isolated sector of life has become unthinkable. This is why I often say that for me there is no such thing as 'profane literature'. All good books, whether they be literary, philosophical, or scientific; whether they describe nature, society, knowledge, or human passions; all of them speak about one thing, that 'one thing needful'. And in general, there does not exist a 'life in itself' which is independent of faith. Ever since my childhood, everything for me has revolved around the Central Principle. To take anything away (with the exception of sin), would be to show ingratitude to God, an unjustified amputation, an impoverishment of Christianity which is called, on the contrary, to penetrate all of life, to give 'life in abundance'. I have always wanted to be a Christian living not by candle light, but in the direct light of the sun."[184]

Fr. Alexander accorded particular attention to culture. He counted many men of culture among his friends and spiritual children. In authentic cultural creation, man actualizes a gift of God. Moreover, is not God Himself called a "most excellent artist" in a text of the Orthodox liturgy? All creative effort can be categorized as an extension of the Divine work.

However, work must not become an end in itself; human activity must not degenerate into activism. Our short life is a school for eternity, Fr. Alexander once explained in one of his sermons.[185] Our soul, our person, our conscience, everything that is divine in us must grow and be educated. We must thus avoid letting ourselves be carried along by the flow of existence; we must know how to stop so as to hear the call of God.

Inviting his listeners to recognize all that was beautiful and good in the world, Fr. Alexander did not, however, look at the world through rose-colored glasses; he had a very strong awareness of the existence of evil in the world. Someone once asked him if the devil existed. He answered:

> "Unfortunately, yes. I am not only convinced that he exists, but I think he can be seen as well. There is evil that comes from imperfection, from suffering, from ignorance, from hunger, and from many other causes... But there is also evil having no natural origin: the demonic [lit. *le satanisme*] which is in man and which Dostoevsky tried to describe... Evil is irrational in its very heart... It seems to me that man becomes "satanized", not through the direct infection of evil, at least I have never observed it in that way, but rather by opening his will to dark forces. At the beginning, all sin is agreed to by man, man opens wide the door to Satan, but when Satan gets in and begins to run the show, then we can rightly speak of possession."[186]

If Fr. Alexander called Christians to live in the present and not be nostalgic for the past, he made no effort to sugar-coat the message of the Gospel for them; they had to remain authentic

Christians in their mind and convictions, in their whole life: "I have no sympathy for the efforts to create a 'secular Christianity' that have been raised here and there in the West," he affirmed.

"The path of compromise linked to the name of Bishop Robinson[187] and other 'modernists' does not contain anything 'modern'.[188] All of it is very naive and superficial. These men are simply blinded and bewitched by 'the spirit of the age'. There is absolutely nothing new in all that, and it will pass like every other fashion."[189]

Fr. Alexander called on people not to confuse Tradition and traditions, reminding them that liturgical forms had changed over the centuries and cannot remain immutable:

"The Gospel in no way abolishes religious rites. Ritual is the living flesh of the sacraments, the framework of spiritual life, the rhythm that unites men and sanctifies daily life. It speaks to the very nature of man. A religious rite becomes a threat and a constraint only when it begins to be seen as a thing valuable in itself, when those things pass for divine and eternal which are in fact of earthly origin."[190]

At the same time, the rules established by the Church play somewhat the same role as does the stability of heredity in the life of organisms. No innovation bears fruit if it completely detaches itself from tradition.

Assuming that it does not become an end in itself, discipline is absolutely necessary for spiritual growth. Fr. Alexander did not approve of those Orthodox whose main preoccupation in Lent was to make lists of foods to be eaten and to be forbidden. At the same time, he thought that Roman Catholicism had gone too far in the reduction and mitigation of fasting. It would change its decision, he said.

It is well known that because of the advent of the Communist regime, the Russian Orthodox Church was unable to carry out fully its reform program undertaken at the beginning of this century, and that the very idea of reform had for a long time been compromised by the collusion between the *renovators* and the Bolsheviks. However, the appearance, in a completely de-Christianized environment, of a new generation of believers without any previous Christian culture, once again posed very sharply the problem of reform - especially liturgical reform. In particular, the archaic language (Church Slavonic) used for the celebration of the services and the reading of the epistle and Gospel is as difficult for modern Russians to understand as is Shakespeare's English for modern English speakers. Fr. Alexander was not satisfied with this situation at all. And yet he refused to act on his own, alone, and to take individual initiatives that would not be in line with the regulations of his Church. He thought that in matters of liturgical reform a prudent and reflective attitude should be adopted, that the path of the golden mean should be found.[191]

In general, he was very respectful of the hierarchical principle of the Church, considering that it pertained to the organizational structure of every body having a practical mission in this world.[192] He did not forget that, in the Orthodox Church as in the Catholic, the priest derives his authority from that of the bishop: he was thus concerned to be linked with the episcopate.

Without doubt he was well acquainted with the weakness of his own hierarchy, but he rarely spoke about the subject. He understood the difficulty of the situation under which they worked and seemed to accept the idea of sharing roles: the hierarchy dealt with the civil authorities, accepting compromise to assure the survival of the ecclesiastical institutions, while the priests and laity could play a more active role.[193]

Fr. Alexander was celebrated for his openness to other Christian confessions, and especially towards Catholicism. His ecumenical convictions had been definitively formed as early as 1958, following a long period of reflection and research. The works of Soloviev certainly had a determining influence. The personality of John XXIII, about whom he had read a great deal when he was a student, also produced a lasting impression on him.[194]

He liked to quote the words of Metropolitan Platon of Kiev, who died in 1891: "Our earthly walls of separation do not go up to heaven".

For Fr. Alexander, the divisions between the Churches had been conditioned by political, national, ethno-psychological, and cultural questions. "I have arrived at the conviction that in reality, the Church is one and that Christians have been divided especially by their narrowness and their sins."[195] He considered that Christians should suffer their division as a sin common to everyone, as a disobedience to the will of Christ. This division can be surmounted, not by following the paths of domination, pride, egotism and hate, but in a spirit of fraternal love without which the Christian vocation cannot be realized.[196]

Of course, real unity between Christians would require a miracle. But Fr. Alexander believed in this miracle:

> "For the moment, let us at least overcome lack of understanding, the aggressive feelings and relations we have. If the members of different communities were to get to know each other better, this would inevitably bear fruit."[197]

Unfortunately, not all Christians are able to recognize what is of value in other confessions. Those whose faith is not very sure, who feel the ground moving under their feet, prefer turning in on themselves. One day, a young man who had begun to attend Baptist assembly meetings asked Fr. Alexander for advice. He did not try to dissuade the young man, and explained to him that he could remain Orthodox while still being open to other confessions. "Oh, but that is really uncomfortable", replied the young man, who finally became a Baptist. Fr. Alexander commented:

> "You see, this young man could only be a Baptist who could not recognize the Orthodox, or an Orthodox who condemned the Baptists. He needed his little shelter. There is a psychological illness called *agoraphobia*: the fear of space. It seems that Tsar Peter the Great suffered from this. He always built himself little houses, little rooms. Well, this sickness also exists in the history of religions!"[198]

He told this story in the last interview that he gave, some days before his murder. He added that recently two or three people had left his parish to become Catholics. The journalist then asked him if he himself had ever considered this possibility. He answered with a lapidary statement: "For me, the Church is one. I think that it would be meaningless."[199]

Fr. Alexander did not approve of going from one Christian confession to another and considered that interconfessional problems could not be resolved by such individual undertakings. He observed, in addition, that: "the great, living centers of Catholicism were outside[200], notably in the Baltic countries, and that in Russia, going over to Catholicism did not permit one to enter into an active ecclesiastical life".[201]

The obstacles put in place by the civil powers hindered believers of different Christian denominations from getting together on a regular basis, and the long-established initiatives undertaken in the West to promote Christian unity were obviously impossible in the USSR. It was only on an individual basis that Christians belonging to different confessions could meet.

Certain spiritual children of Fr. Alexander took advantage of their vacations on the Baltic to meet a Lithuanian Catholic priest, Fr. Stanislas. Fr. Jacques Loew, during his stays in Moscow, took advantage of the May Day celebrations, when the police were normally less vigilant, to conduct Bible study groups in which some of Fr. Alexander's parishioners took part. In this way, Fr. Jacques Loew and Fr. Alexander got to know one another. Fr. Alexander knew that there was no ulterior motive of Roman Catholic proselytism in Fr. Jacques, who in fact encouraged the new converts he met to deepen and fully live their own Orthodox tradition, the unalienable wealth of the one Church. Fr. Alexander also met Little Sister Magdalene who, following in the footsteps of Charles de Foucauld, founded the Fraternity of Little Sisters of Jesus whose model of life is that of Jesus in the poverty and hiddenness of Bethlehem and Nazareth. Sister Magdalene wanted her fraternity to be in touch with men and women all over the world, and having no other means of transportation, she made several trips to Russia in a van, stopping in campgrounds and praying in churches. She found Fr. Alexander on her way.

Finally, the ecumenical community of Taize, founded by the Protestant pastor Roger Schultz, which had created a large youth movement around the world, tried to establish links with the East. In this way, youth and brothers from Taize entered into contact with Russian Christians, notably with the spiritual children of Fr. Alexander, during the seventies. Fr. Alexander was himself personally interested in the Taize experience, both on account of his ecumenical concerns and because of his commitment to youth.

Fr. Alexander counted many Jews among his spiritual children. The number of Jews in the new generation of Christians in the USSR during the seventies was quite astounding. It must be pointed out that, along with the Russians, those of other nationalities who converted during this period had not received a religious formation and had been raised in an atheistic milieu. Often, their connection with the Jewish people was purely ethnic, or was reduced to nothing more than a notation on their identity card. Every Soviet citizen had an internal passport which noted, in the fifth paragraph, the nationality of the bearer: Russian, Ukrainian, Uzbek, Tartar, etc. Or Jew. It was often as a consequence of this inscription marked on their passport that certain Jews began to become aware of their national origin. People often said euphemistically that so-and-so was unable to get into university because of paragraph five, that so-and-so had problems at work because his paragraph five was not in order... Under Brezhnev, anti-Semitism, under the cloak of anti-Zionism, became part of the struggle against the "capitalist and imperialist camp"; it became, in effect, a component of the official ideology.

Along with this, in certain circles wishing to re-animate Russian nationalism, there arose the notion that the excesses of the Revolution could be imputed to the Jews: a distinction was drawn between the good Bolsheviks (the Russians), and the bad communists (the Jews)! According to Fr. Alexander, such anti-Semitism arose from the desire of one part of Soviet society to wash their hands of any responsibility for the crimes of the regime and to blame everything on scapegoats. They had to find a group of people whom they could hold responsible for the sins of the whole of society, who would personify them.

Fr. Jacques Loew

with little sister Magdalen

Fr. Stansilas

The example was given of the demolition, during the thirties, of the great church of Christ the Savior in the center of Moscow. It was always mentioned that the order to blow it up had been given by Kaganovich, a Jew who was one of Stalin's men. Nevertheless, the people did nothing to oppose it and had in fact participated in the destruction of thousands of other churches. They had their share of culpability. But their part was difficult to recognize. It was necessary to find someone guilty, and the Jews made an ideal target.[202]

However things may have been, the results of atheistic education were such that religion and nationality were no longer linked as in the past. Just as Russians were no longer born Orthodox, so the name "Jew" was no longer a synonym for an adherent of Judaism. And if before the Revolution a baptized Jew automatically became Russian, this was no longer so in the present.

Nonetheless, not all baptized Jews felt at ease in Russian Orthodoxy because of its strongly national character and also because of the anti-Semitism of one element of the clergy. Certain of them found a way out in Catholicism. It is evident that Fr. Alexander, due to his general orientation as much as to his origins, was closer to these converts than was anyone else. He deeply loved his Church; the country of his birth; the Russian culture to which he owed so much and with which he fully identified; Russian sanctity, including St. Sergius, St. Seraphim of Sarov, Saint Tikhon of Zadonsk, Russian icons, and the great Russian religious thinkers. And at the same time, he fully assumed his belonging to the Jewish people and saw in this an "unmerited gift".[203]

"For a Jewish Christian", he used to say, "the blood relationship with the prophets, the Virgin Mary, the Savior Himself," was "a great honor and the sign of a double responsibility, as a member of the Church and as a member of the chosen people".[204] To his way of thinking, a Jewish Christian did not cease to be a Jew, but became even more aware of the spiritual vocation of his people. By passing from unbelief to Christian faith, he was brought back to the Bible, to the tradition of his fathers. A Jew confessing Judaism was linked to a baptized Jew by faith in the one God, by the Scripture, by the same religious ethic; while with an atheistic Jew he shared nothing but bloodline.[205]

He affirmed that Israel had been born less as a nation than as a religious community, and that it was constituted more as a Church than as a race. Christianity had enlarged the boundaries of this "Church" to permit all peoples to enter it.[206]

If the majority of Jews had not adopted Christianity, this was no more than another chapter in the unfolding drama between God and men. Christ Himself had lamented over Jerusalem: "You did not know the time of your visitation".[207]

"This drama began in Biblical times. It has also been experienced by other peoples. Indeed, many from among them have abandoned Christianity. I am happy to be able to use my feeble forces to serve the God of Israel and His Church. For me—and this is an unquestioned element of Christian theology— the Old and the New Testaments are inseparable."[208]

The Understanding of
the Faith

CHAPTER 9

Near the grave of Vladimir Soloviev in 1962

"Him (i.e., Christ) we proclaim, warning every man and teaching every man in all wisdom, that we may present every man mature in Christ", said St. Paul.[209] This desire to instruct, making use of all occasions and utilizing every means that presented itself, was at the center of Fr. Alexander's pastoral work.

He taught tirelessly by means of his sermons, his innumerable interviews and conversations with all those who came to see him, and his regular meetings with his parishioners. One of the objectives of the lay groups he set up was precisely to teach.

In addition, he extended his oral teaching with a written instruction just as abundant. Someone once asked him which was more important, his pastoral ministry or the writing of his books. He responded that he was unable to separate the one from the other.[210] His books were one of the forms of his ministry. It was not possible to talk all the time. It was equally necessary to communicate with people in writing. "A book is like an arrow shot from a bow. While you are resting, it is still working for you."[211] Truth to tell, Fr. Alexander hardly ever rested, but he set fly many such arrows which continued their course without him, and continue to do so.

His goal was to destroy the barriers which hindered men from receiving the Word of God: barriers erected by culture, prejudice, preconceived ideas, and stereotypes set up in people's minds by atheistic propaganda:

"In my books, I try to help Christians, especially the new ones, discover the basic principles of the Gospel vision and teaching in a language they can understand. The books written among us before the Revolution are unfortunately not always understandable for today's readers. And foreign books are addressed to people of a psychology and experience different from our own. This is why there always exists a need for new books written in our country. This is particularly true for those who have recently started to walk along the path of faith."[212]

Besides, in order to sustain the dialogue with Soviet society and to respond to the questions of atheists, Christians needed to be capable of responding to the challenge of science, which the official ideology proclaimed to be incompatible with religion.

His first book, entitled *The Son of Man*, is the story of Jesus Christ, and was born of conversations with the newly baptized held at the beginning of his priesthood.

During his adolescence, he had begun a story of Christ's life. Later he had returned to this idea when he was a student. He soon realized that the majority of his contemporaries, deprived of all religious culture, were unable to enter directly into the Gospel text; they needed a key. Many people, he remarked, abandoned their reading from the first page due to the long genealogy which figures in the beginning of St. Matthew, and which they found tedious and incomprehensible.[213]

His goal was to present the earthly life of Jesus of Nazareth to the people of today as though they were eye-witnesses of the events. To do this, he made use of all the data of history, archeology, of Biblical criticism, this last itself employed in a critical manner; nevertheless maintaining a vivid style throughout, accessible to the widest possible audience, pointing out the parallels between the realities of our time and those of Palestine in the time of Christ.

From 1959 to 1962, excerpts from this book appeared in separate articles in the *Journal of the Moscow Patriarchate*, to which for a long time Fr. Alexander had no access, and the complete text remained for ten years in the form of a handwritten manuscript which he gave his close friends to read, continually reworking it until the day he met a Frenchwoman of Russian descent who had just started to work in Moscow.

Asya Duroff was born in Russia before the Revolution. Her parents emigrated, taking refuge in France, where she completed her studies at St. Mary's School in Neuilly, run by a religious community whose founder had been the mother of Cardinal Danielou. Asya became a Catholic and entered the community, while remaining deeply attached to her native land. In 1964, she joyfully accepted the post offered her at the French embassy in Moscow, where her double culture, her sense of hospitality, and her human warmth soon made her indispensible in the multiple functions of her job, at which she remained for fifteen years. Although all the members of the diplomatic missions, as well as other foreign personnel resident in the Soviet capital, were kept in what amounted to a golden cage (from which the majority made no attempt to escape), Asya Duroff was not content to stay cooped up. After work, she would leave the embassy, nonchalantly passing the guard, who watched not only the building but the comings and goings of the diplomatic personnel, and melt into the anonymous crowd of Soviet citizens. Thanks to her typically Russian appearance, her mastery of the language -her mother tongue, and with the aid of a scarf hastily thrown over her head, she had not trouble losing herself among the crowd, and was thus able to visit her many Russian friends she had gotten to know as times and circumstances permitted. Many of them were recent converts, and she tried to bring them spiritual aid, in a profoundly ecumenical spirit, as she had never seen her entry into the Catholic Church as a rupture with Orthodoxy.

So, one day in 1966, one of these new converts invited her to come to a meeting with Fr. Alexander. He spoke to her for a long time about the spiritual situation and the pressing need for religious books. She began by giving him those books she had brought with her to Moscow among her effects; she later found the means to bring in, secretly, books in Russian printed abroad, in particular through the good offices of another Russian emigre, Irene Posnoff, who lived in Belgium.

At the end of the Second World War, Irene met with some Russians who had just been liberated from German camps, or who had been forced to leave their country by the occupying forces. Most often grouped together in refugee camps throughout Western Europe, these men and women, having just lived through extremely harrowing experiences, were asking themselves many questions of a spiritual nature. Wanting to help these people, Irene Posnoff founded a charitable organization in Brussels that became the Eastern Christian Center, and a publishing house, La Vie avec Dieu.[214] At their request, she published brochures specially adapted to their mentality, largely conditioned by the atheistic propaganda with which they had been beaten over the head since their childhood and youth. Thus, for fifteen years after the war, Irene Posnoff worked for these refugees from the Soviet Union who were living in the West.

ASYA DUROFF IN MOSCOW

In 1958, she had occasion to enter into contact with Soviets authorized to attend the Brussels International Exposition, and as a result, she realized that it was for readers living in the USSR itself that her publications were destined. She then undertook the whole effort of translating and publishing, a work entirely inspired by her devotion, tenacity, and faith. Belonging to an Orthodox family - her father had been a professor at the Kiev Theological Academy -, she had also become a Catholic, and in the same spirit as Asya Duroff, without renouncing the Eastern tradition in any way and deeply hoping for the unity of the Churches. Moreover, she worked from the beginning with a Russian Orthodox emigre priest in France.[215] While affirming its Catholic identity, the Eastern Christian Center strove to publish works which could respond to the needs of the Orthodox. It was one of the pioneers of ecumenism.[216]

Irene's new orientation obliged her patiently to seek the means of getting published books into the Soviet Union, of necessity in a clandestine manner. And they did get in, despite the obstacles, to the great displeasure of the official propagandists of Soviet atheism. [217]

Soon assisted by a Slovenian Eastern Rite Catholic priest, Fr. Antoine Ilc, Irene Posnoff quietly accomplished a considerable amount of work. At the end of the eighties, the Center's catalog comprized more than one hundred titles. Among their most important accomplishments were a Russian Bible and New Testament, containing introductions, commentaries, and notes, taken for the most part from the Jerusalem Bible, and enriched by supplementary contributions.

So, through the intermediary of Asya Duroff, Fr. Alexander began to receive the books of the Eastern Center, and entered into correspondence with Irene Posnoff. As soon as she learned of the existence of his book on Christ, she suggested that it be published. At that time, authors who could not be published in the USSR had begun sending their manuscripts to the West. People might not have known much more than the names of Pasternak and Siniavsky, nevertheless, they had heard about the scandal they had provoked. Solzhenitsyn himself did not yet have any contact with Western editors. It was only later that this practice spread. Asya Duroff took charge of getting Fr. Alexander's manuscript through. It was decided to publish it under a pseudonym, and so it was that in 1968, *the Son of Man* finally appeared in print. This was the beginning of a long collaboration between Fr. Alexander and the Eastern Center which afterwards published all his other works.

"I wrote without hope of being published", he confided later. "I am all the happier that all these books have been published and so well edited."[218]

The Center also published books recommended by him, or prepared under his direction.

He remarked one day that hundreds, just from among his personal acquaintances, had received needed spiritual nourishment, thanks to the Center. One of his parishioners used to tell the following riddle: "Question: 'Where are spiritual children born?' Answer: 'Among Brussels sprouts.'"

Through the years, Asya Duroff was the liaison between the Center and Fr. Alexander. Moreover, at the end of the sixties, Fr. Alexander brought Asya into contact with Solzhenitsyn, not directly, as this would have compromised the whole operation, but through several intermediaries. Thus was put in place the first sure and regular pipeline permitting the harried author communication with the West. Asya then began to smuggle out, not only Fr. Alexander's manuscripts, but also those of Solzhenitsyn, an act much more compromising.[219]

The Son of Man had a considerable impact. For many, it was just the right key to unlock the meaning of the Gospel. Fr. Alexander's next book was published by the Eastern Center in Brussels in 1969, this time anonymously; it was an introduction to the Orthodox liturgy, entitled *Heaven on Earth*.[220]

Around 1960, Fr. Alexander had begun a great history of man's religions, which was to comprise six volumes joined under the common title: *In Search of the Way, the Truth, and the Life*. His idea took its inspiration from Vladimir Soloviev, who considered the analysis of ancient religions to be indispensable to the understanding of universal history in general and of Christianity in particular.

When Christ appeared to man, mankind had already traveled a very long road, in the course of which it had become distanced from God, but even so, it had searched for God "gropingly", in the words of St. Paul in his discourse before the Areopagus in Athens. The great religions and ancient philosophy formed a sort of prelude to the New Testament, preparing the world to receive the Gospel.

Centered on the revelation of God in the person of Jesus "crucified for us under Pontius Pilate", Christianity cannot be considered to be merely a simple stage in the spiritual process, even less a synthesis of philosophical and religious systems. Even so, Christianity gave a response to the expectations, to the aspirations of the majority of them. And so it is that the strongest element of Christian spirituality is not negation, but its capacity to encompass, to transcend, to bring to fullness:

"In the same way that white absorbs all the colors of the rainbow, so the Gospel encompasses the faith of the prophets, the thirst for salvation in Buddhism, the dynamism of Zarathustra and the humanity of Confucius. It consecrates the best in the ethics of the philosophers of Antiquity and the mysticism of the sages of India. In doing this, Christianity is not a new doctrine, but rather the announcement of a real fact , of an event accomplished on two levels, the terrestrial and the celestial. Happening in one place and time, it transcends temporal limits. All roads lead to it. It is by its light that the past, present, and future are evaluated and judged. Every movement towards the light of communication with God is, even if accomplished unconsciously, a movement towards Christ." [221]

To study the religious history of mankind before Christianity is not to forget about the problems of today. Fr. Alexander saw a resemblance between the religious quest of his contemporaries and the march of our ancestors towards the knowledge of God. To show how men of former times had searched for God can enlighten the people of today. In addition, every time people have moved away from Christ after the Christian revelation, they always come, in the final analysis, to some doctrine or belief from the past: to Buddha, Confucius, Zarathustra, Plato, Democritus, or Epicurus. Among Christians themselves, there is all too often a resurgence of a pre-evangelical mentality. This is not surprising. Man's past is counted in hundreds of centuries, and two thousand years is too short a time for men to have assimilated the Gospel in its fulness. Fr. Alexander was convinced that Christianity had only taken its first steps, that the Church was only at its beginning stage, that much more time was needed for the leaven of the Gospel to raise all the dough.

If Soloviev had only been able to trace out the main lines of his project without being able to bring it to fruition, Fr. Alexander succeeded in doing just that. One cannot help but be struck by the magnitude of his knowledge, especially when one considers the conditions under which he worked, without ever interrupting his pastoral activity, and of his difficulty in acquiring foreign books, especially the most recent ones. He strove to give his readers, deprived as they were of all religious literature, the maximum amount of information, always writing in a clear style accessible to non-specialists. His work was distinguished for its synthetic character. It did not present the different religions separately, one after another in a static way, but rather tied them together in a general movement in which even the eastern religions, each in their own way, participated. It offered a continuous narrative of man's spiritual saga in its march along the paths of Truth, sometimes advancing, sometimes falling back, sometimes falling headlong into an impasse, in the same way as had the people of Israel in the history of their relations with God.

At the end of the sixties, Fr. Alexander had completed the first five volumes, which were published in Brussels from 1970 to 1972, under a new pseudonym.

The first volume, *The Sources of Religion*,[222] constitutes a general introduction to the whole series and attempts to define the nature of religious phenomenon. At a time when the question of the "death of God" was everywhere discussed, and when Christians in the West prepared themselves to evangelize people completely atheistic, without any religious motivation, Fr. Alexander affirmed, on the contrary, that those who spoke of the "decline of religion" were either short-sighted, or else had voluntarily closed their eyes to reality, or finally, were victims of disinformation.[223] Reviewing all the great recent scientific theories, he demonstrated that there is no incompatibility between faith and science, but that they are two modes of the acquisition of knowledge, which not only should not ignore each other, but which mutually complete and enlighten each other on the path of Truth.

The second volume, *Magic and Monotheism*,[224] described the spiritual evolution of humanity from the dawn of history. Throughout the length of prehistory, belief in magic predominated. For Father Alexander, there existed a direct link between the development of magic and original sin, that initial rupture between man and God. The belief in magic supposes that men have the power to command higher powers to obey them, making men to be "like gods". In reality, this belief rendered them prisoners of unchangeable magic rites, whose proper execution was considered necessary for the continuance of the world, but which long held human creativity paralyzed. However, during the second millennium before Christ, in the Far East as in the Near, men began to free themselves little by little from beliefs founded on magic, while among the people of Israel there appeared faith in one single God.

The three volumes following deal with the spiritual "revolution" instigated during the first millennium before Christ in Greece and China, by the great prophets, philosophers and religious reformers, whose influence is still felt today.

Magic, with its self-seeking goal, gave way to mystical contemplation. India and Greece sought out the path to God by means of ecstasy, abstract thought, the renunciation of the world; Iran and Israel, through confidence in the Creator. The absolute value of earthly goods war brought into question, even totally rejected. Sometimes, as in India, this manifested itself in a fierce struggle against the whole carnal world of the senses.

The majority of the great spiritual masters revised the belief in the cosmic role of ritual and placed morality at the foundation of religious practice.[225] It is the doctrines of this period which water the roots of the social utopias, totalitarian ideologies and atheism which mark the contemporary age.

The third volume, *At the Gates of Silence*,[226] deals with the spirituality of China and India, and the fourth, *Dionysos, the Logos, and Destiny*,[227] with Greek philosophy. As for the fifth, *The Messengers of the Kingdom of God*,[228] it deals with the Biblical prophets from Amos to the return from Babylon. Through their voices, the religion of the Old Testament attained its fulness. They not only announced the coming of the Messiah, they were also the veritable precursors of the revelation of the Gospel.

The sixth and last volume, *At the Threshold of the New Testament*,[229] only appeared in 1983. With more than eight hundred pages, it is the most voluminous of the whole series. It covers the last three centuries before Christ. While Hellenistic civilization spread across the world following the conquests of Alexander the Great, the heritage of the great reformers was disseminated by their successors -imitators, popularizers, and missionaries- none of whom were comparable to the founders. During this process of assimilation, the great religions and philosophical doctrines revealed their limits and weaknesses, thus eliciting disappointment and reaction. It was, to a certain extent, a period of crisis, which saw the rise of pessimism and scepticism. People were tempted to seek refuge in the past, to restore archaic ritual without, however, falling back into magic. New religious quests came to light.[230] Mankind was in a holding pattern until the arrival of the "fullness of time".[231]

The more than ten years which went by between the publication of the first five books and the completion of the last, can no doubt be explained by the breadth of the subject, and equally by the intensification of Fr. Alexander's pastoral activity during the seventies.

During this time, he composed a reader's guide to the Old Testament, *How to Read the Bible*,[232] published in Brussels in 1981 under his own name. He also wrote commentaries on different books of the New Testament destined for inclusion in an edition of the Bible prepared by the Eastern Center in Brussels.

Fr. Alexander accorded great importance to the knowledge of the Bible, and his history of religions must be read in close connection with the Bible. He never stopped his work with the Bible, and was a pioneer in the field; introducing modern Biblical science into his country. The situation of the Church after the Revolution had arrested the normal development of theological research, leaving the question of the interpretation of Holy Scripture largely open; a fundamentalist reading is therefore widely practiced. For his reliance on the data of critical exegesis, Fr. Alexander became the target of numerous attacks from both laymen and priests, from which he regularly had to defend himself.

The last great work he had time to finish before his death was a seven-volume dictionary of Biblical studies, as yet unpublished. This work contains articles on the various Biblical commentators, from Philo of Alexandria through the Fathers of the Church to contemporary authors. There are articles on the main schools and tendencies of exegesis and methods of interpretation, on the history of translations and editions of the Bible, etc. His goal was to provide an instrument that would serve to renew Biblical science in Russia.[233]

Fr. Alexander did not forget the children, and prepared an illustrated album for them, *Where Does All This Come From?*,[234] published in Italy. In order to awaken faith and teach the catechism, he always made use of lively means, as effective for the great as for the small. He used catechetical workbooks prepared by Fr. Loew, which he had come across by accident long before he had met their author,[235] and then worked up his own material, finally producing a whole series of slide shows. Obviously, there is nothing very surprising in this for someone from the West, but in the context of Soviet society, such a catechism was very inventive indeed. At the beginning, the technical quality was quite primitive, but with the help of friends from abroad, this situation improved. More precisely, he had at first simply made use of colored slides in a projector, with a tape recorder playing a recorded text.

The slide show which had the greatest success was entitled: "In Jesus' Steps". Fr. Alexander used slides taken from the Zefirelli film *Jesus of Nazareth*. The slides had been made with the help of a French priest, a friend of the Eastern Center in Brussels, Fr. Jean-Marie Onfroy,[236] who gathered together the illustrations. The owner of a photo laboratory, another Frenchman, Jacques Rousse, reproduced thousands of copies for nothing. These prints were circulated throughout the Soviet Union, were recopied locally, especially by Baptists, and had a considerable impact.

Fr. Alexander loved the movies very much. He often repeated laughingly to his wife that, in him, the world had lost a great cinematographer.[237] "All my dreams have come true", he told a journalist in 1989, when he was no longer bridled by political constraints, "save one—movie making!" "I am completely serious", he added later on. "I would like to make a series of documentary films on the basic tenets of Christianity. My ideal is to make a film on the Bible, both documentary and artistic. I believe that it will happen, one way or another." [238] This was without doubt one of the important works he had yet to accomplish, but death prevented him from realizing his plan.

IRENE POSNOFF BETWEEN TWO COWORKERS
FR. CYRIL KOZINA AND FR. ANTONY ILC

THE KGB PRISON IN MOSCOW

The Time of Testing

CHAPTER 10

AFTER AN INTERROGATION

Дорогие друзья, спасибо за память. Болезнь моя, которая угрожающе прогрессирует, есть просто есть слепота глухота. Лекарств от неё нет, поехать в заграничный рай возможности тоже нет (да и желание особенно нет). Остаётся верить, надеяться и жить дальше. Рад что у вас всё благополучно. Мед. инстанции много времени и мы уважаем силы. Я несмотря на болезнь, усиленно работаю (в частности над слепой библией). Не помню, я кажется

"My illness is progressing in quite a menacing way."

Fr. Alexander always refrained from committing any rash acts that would compromise his spiritual children and call his pastoral ministry into question. He once wrote in a letter, "What counts", he said in a letter, "is to work patiently, tirelessly, in depth".[239] Some dissidents were numbered among his friends and spiritual children, but he kept himself aloof from the political struggle:

> "Obviously, I respect honesty and courage. But I consider that, as far as I am concerned, what I have to do is sufficient. Moreover, I am convinced that liberty must be born out of the spiritual depths of man."[240]

For him, Christians needed to begin by reforming their own lives. The Church was not yet ripe for freedom, was not yet ready to bear witness. She thus needed to concentrate on her internal problems rather than on her relation to the State.

Fr. Alexander's precautions, however, could not keep him out of the eye of the police. In 1964, he barely escaped being sent to prison, and the authorities could not help but be informed about his growing influence. Thus he was always the object of surveillance. At regular intervals, the KGB sought a pretext to make an end of his activities, without ever really realizing their extent.

Fr. Alexander was not in good graces in Church circles, either. His talent was such as to provoke jealousy. Besides, Soviet society was distinguished by a powerful conformity: if someone behaved differently from everybody else, if someone displayed a spirit of independence, that person appeared to break the solidarity of the collective in its submission to the system.

The pastors for whom Fr. Alexander worked as vicar dealt with him in various ways. The first one at Novaya Derevnia took a liking to him. Another let him do what he wanted. A third one, on the contrary, attempted to put a stop to his ministry with new converts. Some, like his pastor in Tarasovka, went so far as to send letters of denunciation. After that, the order went out by word of mouth among Fr. Alexander's spiritual children: 'make your visits to Novaya Derevnia less frequent, don't come to see Father in his office for a little while'.

It was obviously necessary not to trust the members of the parish council (the infamous "twenty"), generally in the pay of the administration. He also had to watch his tongue in the izba attached to the church, as not all the choir members and cleaning ladies were equally trustworthy.

At times, the KGB sent its agents to listen to Fr. Alexander's sermons, with the end of uncovering something subversive, but this was a futile exercise, however, as Fr. Alexander always spotted the "visitors" right away.

Throughout the length of his ministry, Fr. Alexander received anonymous, menacing letters. Informers regularly denounced him to the authorities.

His Jewish origins were not unrelated to the attacks directed against him.

In 1975, a small typewritten Jewish magazine, *The Jews in the USSR*, a samizdat publication passed from hand to hand, published an interview with Fr. Alexander on the relations between Jews and Christianity. It was reprinted by the Paris-based Russian Orthodox publication, *The Messenger of the Russian Christian Movement*.[241] In fact, this "interview" consisted of Fr. Alexander's answers, given in an impromptu and informal manner, to questions posed to him after a Church service. This publication provoked a tempest of criticism. He affirmed justly that he had never suffered personally from any manifestation of anti-Semitism directed at him within the Church. He confirmed this only a few days before his death, saying more precisely that the previous statement had been true up to the end of the seventies, but that after that, things had changed radically.[242]

A new campaign developed against him. A long, anonymous, and libelous letter was put in circulation:

"You do not know me, Fr. Alexander, but I have been observing you for a long time... You are going to have to explain yourself for good, Fr. Alexander... The visible and invisible forces that direct you... Judaism carefully hides from the Jewish people that at the heart of that religion is the worship of Satan... You are a beachhead of Zionism within the Orthodox Church... Infecting the Orthodox with the spirit of Catholicism... The close links between Zionism and Catholic authorities, etc., etc.,"

A more elaborate text attacking Fr. Alexander for his attitude regarding Catholicism and Judaism was sent many times to the civil and religious authorities: the author, always anonymous, plainly knew information inaccessible to ordinary people.

During sermons in the nearby church of Pushkino, the pastor publicly warned his parishioners against his colleague. Soon after, petitions circulated against Fr. Alexander.

Later, another more insidious calumny made its appearance. "Oh, oh! Have you noticed? For all these years, Fr. Alexander has published his books abroad, and nothing has happened to him. Do you believe that it could be possible that...? Fr. Alexander...? is a general in the KGB?" This was a game that these gentlemen loved to play: to spread around the idea that their adversaries were, in reality, collaborators. The KGB had done the same with Solzhenitsyn!

Fr. Alexander did not permit himself to be contaminated by this atmosphere. He kept quiet about these things, so as not to disturb his friends and spiritual children.

Someone asked him one day: "When we cannot escape from those who do us harm, how can we quench the hate in ourselves, the desire for vengeance, so that we might not fall into the trap of resentment and rancor?" He answered:

"We must think, not of the one who has offended, but of Jesus Christ. As soon as the thought of the offender insinuates itself in our spirit, it must be chased away. We must turn toward the clouds, toward the stars, and establish in our selves the same calm found in those heights. We must consider the situation from afar, from above, as if we were dead and were looking at our life from another world...We must not get caught up in conflicts."[243]

Fr. Alexander knew how to adapt himself to the situation and could sense the movement of the political pendulum. When he felt a threat approaching on the horizon, he took extra precautions to protect his groups, notably in asking them to have less frequent meetings, or to suspend them entirely until the storm passed.

For example, he sensed the coming of the flurry of arrests in 1979-1980. In May of 1979, the Central Committee had held a plenary meeting on "ideological work". At the time, no one gave it much thought. He, however, immediately sensed that this did not bode well for believers.

He himself was taken in for interrogation, but spared in the end.

To the attacks from outside were added disappointments caused by certain of his spiritual children to whom he was particularly devoted and to whom he had especially given of himself, who broke with him under the pretext that he did not go far enough, or that he had gone too far..., Were they motivated by a desire for self-affirmation that pushed them, according to Freud, to "kill their father", to do away with him? Had he placed too much hope in personalities too fragile, too vulnerable?

In spite of the weight of the many lives he carried on his shoulders, in spite of the difficulties, in spite of the permanent threat of the KGB hanging above his head like a sword of Damocles, in spite of the disappointments, Fr. Alexander remained unperturbably joyful.

In relation to this, one of his friends recalled the reflection of Nietzsche, who said that the very facial expressions of Christians denied the credibility of their faith. To look at them, he said, one could never guess that Christ had really redeemed them, really freed them. 'Well', the friend continued, 'Nietzsche could never have said that about Fr. Alexander!'[244] His was not a sad Christianity. He even wanted to do a study on the humor of Christ.[245] His gaiety was not due only to his character. It seems that he had been subject to bouts of melancholy in his childhood. [246] His gaiety was the result of work on himself; it was nourished by his deep faith and by his intimacy with Jesus Christ. It enabled him to forget the conditions in which he exercised his ministry. He seemed to be gifted with an extraordinary faculty of self-renewal. Sometimes, he would arrive at a friend's house, tired and worn out, but in only a minute a smile would come back to his face and he would once again communicate his energy to those present, like a battery that recharged itself instantaneously. A doctor friend confided:

> "It seemed that in the powerful music of his life, he exercised no self-control, that obstacles overcame themselves, but this was not the case at all. Few people knew that his physical state was far from being ideal. When one examined him, one wondered how his organism could hold up. His inexhaustible energy was not physical, it was earthly only in appearance. It was really of a very different nature."[247]

During the years that followed the death of Brezhnev, there was a general tightening of the screws throughout the Soviet structure. His successor, Andropov, was an expert; having spent almost fifteen years as head of the KGB, he attempted to solve the country's problems by means of force. The repressive arsenal was again increased. The penal code was modified in such a way that the courts could find additional reasons to condemn dissidents and to arbitrarily prolong the sentences of those already imprisoned. Various measures were adopted making it a crime for Soviets to have contact with foreigners. The conditions in the detention camps were aggravated. Stronger and stronger pressure was exercised on political prisoners to renounce their former activities. The country once again slid into a state of fear.

In 1983, the Central Committee of the Communist Party launched a vigorous campaign against believers and called for an intensification of atheistic propaganda. The KGB launched a new offensive against active Christians.

The net also tightened around Fr. Alexander. In that year there was arrested one of his former spiritual children, who had broken with him some years before in order to become Catholic. Later on, this same man had been secretly ordained a Catholic priest and had gathered a small community around himself. In the sinister prison of Lefortovo, he cracked and confessed many things which compromised a number of those near Fr. Alexander, as well as Fr. Alexander himself. This time, the KGB seemed determined not to let go of its prey.

He was summoned to interminable daily interrogations, to which he went as if to work. At various times, not seeing him come out, people believed he had been arrested. Many seizures took place at Novaya Derevnia and Semkhoz. All activities had to be put on hold. It was then that he began work on his Biblical encyclopedia. It was a work that he thought would be useful in Russia, and which demanded less tranquillity of spirit than other works.[248]

His friends asked among themselves if he ought not leave the country. But he never approved of those who tried to emigrate. To a man of letters who came to him immediately before becoming an expatriate, he said: "A writer must live in his own country. Manuscripts may go here and there as they want, but our place is here. People are waiting for the Word."[249] The flood of emigration had practically stopped at that moment, but the KGB would not have been unhappy to see Fr. Alexander leave.

To his friends abroad who had asked him how they could help, he responded with a hastily written note in his practically illegible hieroglyphic script, with its usual rising lines, though this time not rising quite so high. He wrote in code, in case the message should fall into hostile hands, though not without humor, in spite of the gravity of the situation:

> "My illness, which is progressing in a menacing manner, is only a part of the general epidemic. No remedy exists. To move to another less infested region is impossible, and not something I particularly want to do. All that can be done is to believe, to hope, and to continue to live."[250]

The 'illness' obviously meant the risk of being arrested, and the 'epidemic' was the policy of repression, which was then intensifying.

One effort was undertaken, however, by Pastor Maury, the president of the Protestant Federation of France and member of the central committee of the World Council of Churches, who addressed a letter to the president of the Council on Religious Affairs in the USSR.

Fr. Alexander had a profound confidence in Providence. He knew well that God can write straight with crooked lines. How many times he repeated: "If God wills! When God wants...! No, all his spiritual children were there in the USSR, and he could not abandon them. His humility also helped him to endure his trials, and he thought of the fate of his predecessors in the faith:

> "In my youth, I had a spiritual father, Fr. Piotr Shipkov,[251] who spent thirty years in the camps or in confinement. When I think of everything he suffered, it is difficult for me to speak about what has hapZpened to me. I will say this: in the difficult years, I learned to count the value of each

minute. I give thanks to God that He has allowed me to serve for four decades without interruption."[252]

Fr. Alexander finished by addressing a letter of explanation to the ecclesiastical authorities, as well as another to the Council of Religious Affairs.

Designated the head of the Communist Party in March 1985, Gorbachev seemed at first to want to carry out a policy of getting the country back on its feet through the reinforcement of discipline. Over the course of 1986, however, he sent several signs to intellectuals, and the vise of cultural censorship began to loosen, though in the religious domain, the previous policy was pursued without change. Thus, in September 1986, *Pravda* once again dedicated an editorial to the reinforcement of atheistic propaganda, as it had done each year at about the same time since 1983.

Fr. Alexander's trials had not come to an end. In 1984, another of his former spiritual children was arrested; Fr. Alexander had separated himself from this man, as his activities had put the whole parish in danger. The man had shown great courage under interrogation and during the trial, at which he was accused, among other things, of exercising a religious influence on his friends and of distributing religious books to them. It was in camp that he broke. He appeared on television at the beginning of 1986, his head shaved and his face emaciated, confessing to have been involved in a "political activity criminal under the State and harmful to the Church". Previously, he had sent an interminable and incoherent letter to Fr. Alexander, written in a frightful gibberish and obviously inspired by men in uniform "only thinking of his own good". He invited Fr. Alexander to investigate the "positive elements" of communism, and went on to denounce (and it is here that the cloven hoof of the KGB was revealed): the organization of small groups, the reading of religious books published abroad, and the use of slides and tape recorders for catechesis—all of which were illegal and contrary to the teaching of the Church!

And then, in April 1986, the periodical Trud published a long article attacking several Orthodox Christians: Alexander Ogorodnikov, then in prison; Fr. Gleb Yakunin, exiled in Siberia; and even Fr. John Meyendorff,[253] dean of St. Vladimir's Seminary in New York. The document was a real "KGB salad", made up of all those ingredients common to that style of literature. Fr. Alexander was also named; being accused of having "organized a religious circle and distributed recordings of dubious content". That October in France, the presidents of the Conference of Catholic Bishops, the Protestant Federation, and the Orthodox Inter-episcopal Committee protested against the article in *Trud* by writing a letter to the Council on Religious Affairs of the USSR.[254] The storm, however, was finally coming to an end.

And regardless of what is thought nowadays of the relations of one element of the Orthodox hierarchy with the Soviet powers, Fr. Alexander remained grateful for the support he received from his own bishop, Metropolitan Juvenaly of Krutitsy, who was in charge of the Moscow region.[255]

It was during this time, on April 26, 1986, that the Chernobyl catastrophe took place, which revealed to the governing powers the dilapidated state of the country, perhaps making them aware that it was no longer possible to remedy the situation solely by means of force.

In December, the celebrated dissident Anatoly Marchenko died in prison, as had six other political prisoners before him since Gorbachev's accession to power. This last event had a great impact, marking the end of the post-Brezhnev winter.

AT SCHOOL #67, OCTOBER 19, 1988

Apotheosis

CHAPTER 11

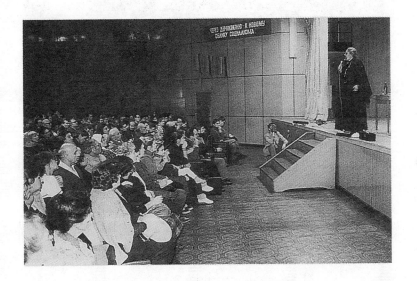

M. Gorbachev receiving Patriarch Pimen.

In the week following Marchenko's death, a telephone was installed in the apartment where Sakharov was under house arrest in Gorky, and Gorbachev called the illustrious academician. The first liberations of political prisoners began after this. Notable among them was Fr. Yakunin. It was not, however, until the end of 1987 that the Soviet authorities made a first gesture toward the Orthodox Church, by announcing the restoration to the Church of two monasteries, notably the one at Optina.

The turning point in Soviet policy in regard to religion came in 1988, when the Russian Orthodox Church celebrated the Millenium of the country's baptism. One of the principal architects of this change in orientation was the new president of the Council of Religious Affairs, Kharchev, a party functionary named to the post in 1985, who little by little discovered the importance of the religious experience. During a secret meeting in March 1988 with the professors of a Soviet leadership training school, Kharchev confided that, despite persecutions, repression, and administrative constraints, religious belief had not diminished, but was in fact increasing.[256]

Kharchev said that each year, for example, one million religious funerals were held. In his opinion, funerals were the surest indicators of religious conviction, since, while living, did not dare to say what they thought out of fear of losing their jobs. "We have the habit", he continued, "of thinking that there are only little old ladies in the churches, but go in yourselves, and you will see adults in the prime of life, men of our generation." He concluded essentially by saying that, if believers could not be eliminated, they should be integrated into the system. What is more, in an article published in the atheistic journal *Science and Religion*, he expressed his satisfaction with the contribution which Church made to society: in encouraging its faithful to be truly professional and not to drink; in strengthening the family; its work for the preservation of national cultural monuments.[257] During the same address, he made allusion to the resistance within the Party to the easing of the policy toward believers. He was thus inundated by telephone calls when Orthodox bishops were shown on television participating in this or that conference. The same thing occurred when he raised to prominence the question of the teaching of the catechism:

"I was rapped on the knuckles. People told me, 'That's all we need: Sunday schools after seventy years of Soviet government! Is your head screwed on straight? What are people going to say?' Please understand me. I am against Sunday schools. But all the same, we have to do something."[258]

After much hesitation, the authorities finally decided to permit the Orthodox Church to commemorate its Millenium with solemnity, and they even took part in it themselves. The signal was given by two events. On April 8, 1988, the eve of Pascha, *Izvestia* published a long interview with Patriarch Pimen, and on April 29, in the Kremlin, Gorbachev received the Patriarch and the highest ranking members of the hierarchy.

For Fr. Alexander as well, these changes announced the end of a long, dark tunnel. Already in 1987, a collection of theological essays had been published by the Patriarchate, which included an article of his on Biblical science in the Russian Orthodox Church.[259] True, it was a very small printing, making it inaccessible to all but a small circle of specialists, but it was the first line of Fr. Alexander's to see print in his own country since 1966. During the Millenium celebrations, he received an ecclesiastical award.[260] Also, for the first time in his life, he was permitted to go abroad: he made a trip to Poland at the invitation of Orthodox friends. These hoped that he would stay a month in order to see the whole country, but Fr. Alexander was in a hurry. What really interested him was the organization of religious education, the publication of religious materials, and the establishment of spiritual retreat centers. He often repeated that there was much to do in Russia and that time was short. At the end of eight days he returned to Moscow.[261]

On May 11, 1988, at the cultural center of the Steel Institute in Moscow, he gave his first public lecture. After a presentation on the Millenium, he answered a series of questions from his audience about the ceremonies and canonizations which were to take place, the organization of the Orthodox Church and its place in society, the relations between science and religion, etc. Such a thing had never been seen before: a priest addressing a group of students and teachers, and in a State school! Without doubt, nothing of the kind had been seen since the 1920s; during that time, public debates had been organized between believers and atheists, and the oratorical jousting that had occurred between the brilliant leader of the renovators and the Minister of Education became part of the collective memory.

The Millenium ceremonies began in Moscow on June 5th. The official character given to the celebration, the fact that the media gave it such wide coverage, amounted to an official rehabilitation of the Church in the eyes of society: she could finally be seen in public, to come out of the marginalization to which she had been confined over the decades. The population got the feeling that, finally, the State was no longer trying to stop them from practicing religion. Many people were baptized that summer; some, no doubt, more out of a desire to keep alive the tradition of their ancestors than as an expression of real conversion.

The press began to publish articles which attempted to describe religious life in an objective manner. More and more often, pictures of churches and religious ceremonies appeared on television. Soon, Church officials were even invited to programs to discuss the question of "spirituality", a mysterious word of which the press would soon get its fill. Churches, monasteries were reopened. The law, however, remained unchanged. Local authorities remained generally hostile. True, the central authorities had made a gesture, but was it not just for the moment? The future was uncertain. During that summer, one of Fr. Alexander's spiritual sons asked him what he thought of perestroika. He answered that he thought it was very positive, for when the hunters hunt each other, the rabbits can play freely! [262] During the summer, he was one of the first to ask that Solzhenitsyn's works be published in Russia, and that his Soviet citizenship, which the author had lost when he was expelled from the country, be restored.[263] It took another year, however, before a magazine could begin to publish extracts from *The Gulag Archipelago*.

In the autumn, Fr. Alexander inaugurated a series of talks at the club of the Krasnaya Presnia, a district of Moscow, on the theme: 'Christianity, History, and Culture". On October 19, there occurred an event even more unheard of: he was invited to speak at a school in the capital. Even the great daily newspaper *Izvestia* reported on it![264] From then on, the frequency of his public appearances increased. Soon, he was being invited several times a week to speak in clubs, cultural centers, and educational institutions. In two years, he must have given around two hundred lectures, including several series on the Bible, the history of the Church, the great religions of man, Russian religious thinkers, and a commentary on the creed.

He would speak wearing the wide-sleeved riassa and large metallic pectoral cross of an Orthodox priest. His trials had peppered his curly hair and neatly trimmed beard with white, but his face remained young, extraordinarily handsome, and radiated sweetness. In his twinkling black eyes both goodness and intelligence could be seen. He spoke in a warm baritone, with some nasal intonations. Without any note or paper, he would move back and forth across the smaller halls, or would walk the length of the stage, carrying a microphone in his hand. His features were ceaselessly in motion, his expressive physiognomy sometimes serious, sometimes lit up by a smile- a smile either tender, or lively, or charming. He always spoke as if he were talking individually to each person. After a lecture on the subject announced, he would usually answer questions from his listeners. Most often, as is done usually in Russia, the questions were written on little pieces of paper and passed up to the stage, where Fr. Alexander unfolded and answered each one. Even when there was not much time left, he spoke on the fundamentals of the most difficult questions for several minutes.

If someone asked him a personal question, he found personal words for the answer. A journalist bears witness. She was present at a meeting with Fr. Alexander in a suburban club; that evening the participants presented their questions by going up on stage, one by one. One very thin woman was telling him all the troubles she had undergone:

"And then Fr. Alexander answered her; I did not hear what he said. He spoke to that woman, and to her alone. By what miracle or acoustical principle can this be explained:

one person alone understood what the priest said.... Only the one that he was addressing."[265]

As for questions "out of the blue", he always found an instantaneous repartee which made the whole audience burst out laughing. An audience hungry to listen to him. But there were other, more provocative, questions, such as: "What are you, a Jew, doing in our Orthodox Church?" He would explain calmly that there is, for a Christian, "neither Jew nor Greek".[266]

Although the country was little by little opening up to a plurality of opinions, those in power had not renounced Communism, the symbols of which were still in place. Thus it was at the "Hammer and Sickle" cultural center that Fr. Alexander gave a series of lectures on the history of religions- a humorous twist of Providence and a sign of the precariousness of the times. Another time as well, he spoke under a banner stretched across the stage which proclaimed: Lenin's work will live forever!

Fr. Alexander twice participated in a debate with atheist propagandists, but these were so insipid, insignificant and dull that no one wanted to repeat the experience.[267]

In October 1988, one of his articles appeared for the first time in a journal other than the Patriarchate's. This publication was followed by thirty others in 1989 and 1990, in the most diverse publications, including widely-circulated magazines. Nonetheless, not one of his books was published in Russia during his lifetime.

There were those who asked, perplexed, why it was that this priest, whom no one had heard of before, was invited to speak everywhere; why his name so regularly appeared on posters and the press, why he had such success, why he had become so suddenly popular. As Fr. Alexander had so often repeated in the past:

"The most difficult moment for the Church will come when everything is permitted us. Then we will be ashamed because we are not ready to bear witness, and unfortunately, we are preparing ourselves very poorly for that moment..."[268]

"When we have something to say, God will give us a platform, even on television."[269]

He, however, was ready. All his pastoral work, all the books he had written, the knowledge he had acquired, had prepared him for this meeting with Soviet society when, at whatever time, conditions would render it possible.[270] But how many others had been surprised by the sudden appearance of liberty, like the foolish virgins of the parable whose lamps were out when the bridegroom they were waiting for finally arrived?

And in fact, television did begin to take an interest in religion. But what did it show? Blue, star-studded cupolas and golden vestments; banners; choirs executing magnificent chants; church officials making unctuous statements, couched in the rhetorical style of the nineteenth century, bombastic and utterly empty.

After seeing one of these shows, Fr. Alexander made this commentary:

"Of course, we should say 'thank you'. Who would have thought that we would see this one day. But all the same, there is little rapport with the faith... The State is disabled. With the aid of the Church, it would like to re-establish certain moral norms. Notice that no one, not even the bishops whom they produce on television, preach Jesus Christ,

God; they don't speak of the essentials of what we believe. The little paintings showing sentimental country scenes with churches, such as are sold on the Arbat[271]-that's what this 'spirituality' consists of. I must say that even that can be cut off from one day to the next. We need to hurry to give people the authentic message of Christ and not a spiritual placebo for the poor."[272]

Fr. Alexander was disquieted by seeing a growing tendency among the clergy toward a conservatism characterized by a nostalgia for the past, hostility to everything foreign, anti-ecumenism, and opposition to any reform. It was a reaction to the destruction of all national values by the Communist regime. What is more, the legitimate desire to recover one's roots, to affirm one's identity was not restricted to the Orthodox. It was also shared by the Catholics of the Soviet Union, even though their Church has a supra-national structure. The development of this preoccupation with identity was fraught with danger. A number of priests were sympathetic to ultra-nationalist movements which reduced Orthodoxy to an attribute of national identity, such as the infamous *Pamyat* movement, violently xenophobic and anti-Semitic, at the same time secretly supported by the KGB.

In idealizing the past, these people forgot that the nineteenth-century Church had its share in responsibility for the catastrophe of 1917, and that, in the decades following, the Soviet authorieties had been only too happy to present the Church as part of the debris of a past world.[273] No, the Church is not a museum! In one of his last sermons, Fr. Alexander expressed his happiness that the State was giving churches back to the faithful, who were restoring them, but, he added: "if we do not convert our hearts, if we do not change our way of life, these buildings will be nothing more than empty shells".[274]

During this time, perestroika was having its ups and downs. In the spring of 1989, a new parliament of the Soviet Union was elected, the Congress of the People's Deputies. These elections did not take place under truly democratic conditions, as the Communist Party continued to be the only real option; however, for the first time since the establishment of the Soviet regime, several candidates were permitted to contest each seat. The first session of this Congress, which opened in the month of June, gave the place a thorough house-cleaning. A certain number of deputies did not hesitate to question the whole Communist system. For fifteen days, life seemed to stop: the whole population was tied to television screens, watching the live broadcast of the sessions. At the same time, a peaceful protest was savagely repressed in Tbilisi,[275] where students on a hunger strike were massacred by men wielding shovels.

With regards to religion, the authorities hesitated once again. In May 1989, the ideological commission of the Central Committee of the Communist Party sent back for study a draft law that would have made life easier for churches and religious associations. The law on freedom of conscience would not finally be adopted until October 1990, a month after Fr. Alexander's death. Kharchev, the president of the Council on Religious Affairs, was removed. The restoration of churches continued, but was frequently held up by local Communist officials. The faithful undertook long hunger strikes to recover places of worship.

In October, the Orthodox Church celebrated the four hundredth anniversary of the founding of the Moscow Patriarchate. For the occasion, a religious service was celebrated, for the first time since 1918, in the Dormition Cathedral of the Kremlin, which had been transformed into a museum after the Revolution. The Patriarchate used the occasion of this commemoration to canonize Patriarch Tikhon, for whom Fr. Alexander had particular veneration and of whom he made regular mention during the liturgy.

That Easter, the Catholic archbishop of Paris, Cardinal Lustiger, made an official visit to the USSR at the invitation of the Moscow Patriarchate. On his way to the Trinity-St. Sergius Lavra, he insisted on stopping at Novaya Derevnia where he was able to speak privately with Fr. Alexander in English.

At the same time, Jean Vanier, the founder of the *l'Arche* communities, which care for the mentally handicapped, went to Russia and made the acquaintance of Fr. Alexander in Moscow. Fr. Alexander had known of the existence of these communities and thought their work to be exemplary. Jean Vanier said that he was very touched by this meeting: "He was a great prophet who had an immense love for Jesus. He was a brave man, for whom, without any doubt, God was the source of life."[276]

At the end of October, Fr. Alexander spent a few days with his daughter, who had just moved to Italy. By an extraordinary coincidence of events, he happened to be in Rome, where he had gone to participate in a conference, at the very moment that little sister Magdalene of Jesus died. He had met her in July on her last visit to Russia. He was happy to be a sort of representative of his Church and of Russia at her funeral, as her example had been of value for everyone. She had shown the power of authentic, Gospel love in the service of all men.[277]

In December 1989, the country was saddened by the death of Sakharov, whose funeral drew a great crowd. In January 1990, tanks rolled into Baku and lay siege to the city. Then there was a new upsurge in favor of democracy, especially after the big protest marches in Moscow and in other large cities of the country. In March, the article of the Constitution dealing with the Party's dominant role in governing the country was amended. Elections designed to renew the parliaments of the republics and all the local assemblies gave the victory to those seeking independence in the Baltic countries, in western Ukraine and elsewhere; in Russia as well, democrats won in a certain number of municipalities, such as Moscow. Fr. Yakunin was also elected deputy to the Russian parliament.

His own bishop, Metropolitan Juvenaly, asked Fr. Alexander why, considering his popularity, he did not run for office himself. "Your Eminence", he replied:

> "When would we have time to be in politics? Today we have the chance to preach the Word of God day and night, and I have given my life completely over to that task."[278]

Although it was not his own path, he nevertheless considered that the exceptional situation of the country justified the engagement of priests in political life. He said:

> "We live in a time when all members of society have to take part in the country's renaissance. When things have returned to normal, such political activity will no longer be necessary."[279]

In July, Boris Yeltsin broadcast his resignation from the Communist Party, which was coming under more and more open criticism. However, Party conservatives[280] were no doubt already planning their revenge, perhaps for the fall.

Patriarch Pimen died that May. A council of Russian Orthodox Church was convoked to choose a successor. Although not determined according to the same principles as the Council of 1917-1918, to whose spirit a number of clergy and laity had called for

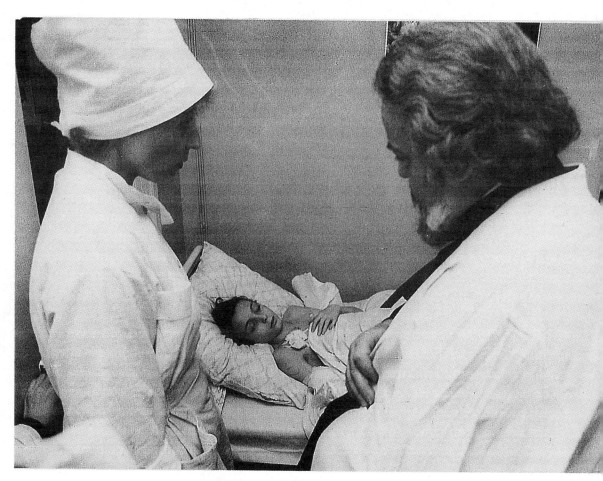

AT THE CHILDREN'S HOSPITAL IN JANUARY 1990

AT A CONFERENCE IN NOVEMBER 1988

a return, the election of the new Patriarch did take place by secret ballot, in contrast to the elections of 1943, 1945, and 1971. Metropolitan Alexei of Leningrad was elected. He had participated in the guidance of the Church for thirty years, with all the ambiguous relations with the Soviet authorities that this implied: the silence, the forced passivity, etc. Metropolitan Alexei seemed to be a cultivated, open man. In 1987, he had been the first among the bishops to speak out against the condition of believers, who were too often treated like second-class citizens.[281] He was also the only one to denounce xenophobia and anti-Semitism. All in all, Fr. Alexander felt that he had been a good choice. At the same time, the council canonized Fr. John of Kronstadt, who had healed Fr. Alexander's great-grandmother.

Nonetheless, divisions appeared in the Church. Some Orthodox, accusing the hierarchy of having compromised themselves with the Communist powers, decided to place themselves under the obedience of the Russian Orthodox Church Abroad, a jurisdiction having its origins in the emigration and currently based in the United States. Its hierarchy appealed to the authorization given to bishops during the Civil War by Patriarch Tikhon. This authorization, in reality given only provisionally, permitted bishops to govern their dioceses autonomously in case of adverse circumstances. The Church Abroad considers itself rightfully to have assumed the heritage of Russian Orthodoxy, in place of the Moscow Patriarchate, the latter which had, in their eyes, completely sold out to a power that was the declared enemy of God.

In an interview with a Spanish journalist four days before his death, Fr. Alexander spoke out against this schism, saying that the position advocated by the proponents of the Church Abroad was tainted with nostalgia for the past. Without trying to cover over the faults of the Orthodox Church, Fr. Alexander re-affirmed that there was no other choice than to remain within the Moscow Patriarchate.[282] On the eve of his death, he said to one of his spiritual daughters:

> "Don't believe anyone who tells you that our Church is not holy. Since the fourth century, people have been lamenting and saying that the end of the Church had come. It is not us, who are sinners, who make the Church live, but our Lord Jesus Christ. He is still here with us in His Church. It is here that the incarnation of Christ continues in history, here that His kingdom is found."[283]

During the course of the spring and summer of 1990, people's desire to be free from Party and State control grew yet stronger. What people called the "informal movement" took on new life. People began to create new political parties, various humanitarian associations, independent newspapers and publishing houses, even private schools. Many of these projects failed, but they abounded nonetheless. Christians also took part in this creative outburst.

This was a time of intense activity for Fr. Alexander as well. From the beginning of the year he had participated, along with other Orthodox, Protestants and Catholics, in the creation of a Bible Society. Later on, he began to lay the foundation for an Orthodox university, in the form of evening classes. He also created an association called Cultural Renaissance, whose goal was both educational and humanitarian. On the one hand, the association organized conferences and various kinds of meetings. On the other, a group of parishioners from Novaya Derevnia took over a service at the Pediatrics Hospital of the Russian Republic in Moscow, where gravely ill children waiting for kidney transplants were cared for. At a time when the entire health-care system was in a disastrous state, these people helped the medical personnel and gave psychological support to the sick children.

What is more, several of Fr. Alexander's spiritual children decided to open a free school, outside the strait-jacket of official programs, and he gave their efforts his support.

At Novaya Derevnia, where he had finally been named rector, construction was begun on a building to serve as both baptistry and parish hall, the plans of which he had drawn up himself. He was unable to finish the project, however, and today a pile of concrete blocks still sits to the left of the church, just beside his grave.

Finally, he organized a Sunday School to teach the catechism to the children of the village, which he opened just a week before his death.

The Baptists organized a big rally in the Moscow Olympic Stadium on Easter of 1990. This type of evangelization is quite foreign to Orthodox sensibilities, and although the Patriarchate was invited to participate, no one went.[284] Fr. Alexander took up the challenge, however. He appeared before the immense crowd, dressed in a white, paschal-colored riassa, and spoke of Christ's Last Supper with his apostles on the eve of His Passion.

A woman journalist produced, along with Fr. Alexander, a whole series of religious programs for children. She had to be very stubborn, however, to get them aired on Russian radio. Fr. Alexander also appeared on several TV shows just before hi death, and was offered a weekly program on one of the networks. He managed to record four segments that were to be broadcast in the fall. After his murder, it was discovered that the tapes had been erased. Could it have been a technical error? An accident? Or is it possible that this project sealed his fate? Imagine the state of mind of the many KGB agents who had spent years watching him, provoking him, trying to neutralize him. Now they saw him speaking to bigger and bigger audiences. All they needed was a regular TV show! "That's it. We've had enough," they may have said to themselves.

In May, Fr. Alexander again went abroad, this time to Germany, where he had been invited to participate in several congresses. From there he went to Brussels, where for the first time he met Irene Posnoff and Fr. Antony Ilc, who had published his books.

On August 15/28, the feast of the Dormition, Fr. Alexander welcomed to his parish Fr. Daniel Ange, who was visiting from France. Fr. Daniel had created centers called Youth Light, in order to prepare young people to evangelize others of their own age. Fr. Alexander was very interested in this project. Fr. Daniel reported that at dinner the two of them had talked about two things more than anything else: 1) the crowds of newly baptized who had not yet been sufficiently instructed in the faith; 2) the evangelization of thousands of young people who knew absolutely nothing about God, but who were nonetheless hungry for spiritual food and were being taken in by esoteric sects.[285]

Certain of Fr. Alexander's friends and spiritual children believed that he was doing too much, fearing that he was physically exhausting himself, that he might get caught up in something he could not control, that he might burn out. Perhaps they were unknowingly a little bit jealous because he was less available to them. He must have felt, however, that he was finally able to give his all to his work. He wrote to a friend:

"It isn't easy to understand someone who for years has been tied up on a leash. I am not complaining for myself, because God has given me the possibility of doing something, even on the end of this leash...

"In fact, I have always had regular meetings with people, just like these. It's only the proportion that has changed. Before, there were thirty people; today, three hundred or more. But the basis is the same, however. The goals are the same. The forms too... I don't prepare myself in any special way; I let God inspire me. And, of course, I can't let people know right away what I want. Things have to go step by step. Nonetheless, the multiplication tables do not do away with higher mathematics. Everything comes in its own time. I don't spend more time in public now than I did during the period of stagnation[286]. It's only the number of listeners that has increased...

"I work now as I have always worked: with my face into the wind. This is not as easy as it may sometimes seem. At the present time, the wind is obviously stronger, especially from the Black Hundreds.[287] I have to stand solidly on my two feet, legs spread, in order not to be overturned. In short, don't be worried about me... I am only an instrument that God is using for the moment. Afterwards, things will be as God wants them."[288]

He seemed haunted by the idea that his was an unrepeatable chance to transmit the message of the Gospel, that time was running out, and that he could not afford to lose an instant:

"At present I am like the sower in the parable. I have been given a unique chance to spread the seed. True, the vast majority of it will fall on rocky ground and will never sprout. You think I don't know what kind of mush people have in their heads? Nonetheless, if after having heard me, only a few people wake up, or even only one person, that's something, isn't it? You know, I have the feeling that this is not going to last long, at least for me.."[289]

On television in January 1989

I met Fr. Alexander for the last time in the month of July 1990. After having received me in his little office, he was the first to leave, pressed for time as he always was. He said goodbye to me, but came back a first time, then a second. Walking off again, he stopped at the threshold. His face illuminated by the radiance of his expression and his good, impish smile, he held up his hand in a V-for victory.

Looking back, I understand this as a message of hope to be received from beyond the grave, as a sign of paschal victory. Such were, in fact, his last public words, spoken on the eve of his murder: "This victory began on the night of the Resurrection, and it will continue as long as the world exists..."

AT THE OLYMPIC STADIUM, PASCHA, 1990

Introduction to the Original French Version

When I found myself face to face with Fr. Alexander Men, I felt I had known him all my life. He seemed like a brother, a friend who would always be close to me, despite the fact that we only spoke for perhaps ten minutes. Let me first tell you about the circumstances of our meeting.

It was during a trip to the USSR at the beginning of May, 1989. I had been invited by the Patriarch of Moscow, and at that time the Soviet government's religious policy was still uncertain. The law on freedom of conscience was then only under study.

Fr. Alexander Men was one of those mystical figures whose light and influence was felt to be a menace by the Communist authority and its police. He was under suspicion by both the KGB and the anti-Semites, and in order to silence him, one or the other group, or both together, had him killed with an axe as he was going to his church.

From that moment on, his words have the ring of authority; they are sanctioned by his martyrdom. No human being can now silence the living words of his assassinated voice. Russia turned its ear to those words when Boris Yeltsin, then president of the Supreme Soviet, called the assembly to a moment of silence for the murdered Fr. Men.

On Saturday, May 6, 1989, my traveling companions and I were on our way from Moscow to the Zagorsk monastery. The night before, I had asked our hosts at the Moscow patriarchate to stop at Novaya Derevnia, the village where Fr. Alexander had his parish; more precisely, he was still the second priest and not yet the pastor. It had been impossible to inform him of our visit. We only knew that he would be happy to receive us and that he would be in church on that day. It was the week after Easter, called Bright Week in the Orthodox Church, and the liturgy would be celebrated in all the churches that were open.

We arrived at the end of the liturgy, during the pastor's sermon; it is customary to preach after the eucharist. My companions and I stayed in the back of the church. Fr. Alexander saw us. The pastor's sermon went on and on, and there was no way to stop him. Fr. Alexander came up to me, and we had a brief conversation in English at the back of the church, just the two of us. The pastor finally finished his sermon and invited me to say a few words and to bless the faithful. Then, because we were pressed for time, we said good-bye and left.

Without ever having met before, we felt we had many things to say to each other but not time to say them. My memory of the event has taken the form of a strong, beautiful vision of a meeting in the mystery of the suffering and raised Messiah, a mystery that we both contemplated together. We exchanged what was essential, and we comforted one another much more than words could say.

From then on, I have tried to explore the wealth of meaning contained in our encounter but have not been able to completely grasp its significance. It was obvious to us, first of all, that our fraternity of faith, that our communion in Christ was like a sign, a foretaste of the full communion in the mutual love and respect of the Patriarch of Moscow and the Church of Rome. When he was speaking of the gifts of the Spirit, St. Paul called such a sign a "guarantee," a "pledge." (2 Cor 5:5) I say "It was obvious *to us*" without any other certitude of being able to speak for Fr. Men than the intuition of that moment which has always remained with me. Both he and I, in fact, by becoming Christian, were loving and serving the one Bride of Christ, His Church.

It was also obvious, however, that His disciples could only live this communion by sharing the mystery of the Cross.

Yet, the joy of that Easter Week, as it illuminated the poor assembly in which Fr. Alexander and I exchanged a few words, was bathed in the mystery of the Cross and colored by the threat of a powerless yet imminent death. The resurrected Christ gives us a freedom that is stronger than all the world's tyrannies. The victory of faith is a victory of deliverance, forgiveness, and love. The weakness of Christ, who was handed over to the power of men, makes God's power appear because it is He who frees us from the power of sin.

Fr. Alexander and I knew all this, and yet, nearly without words, we gave thanks for having found one another, witnesses for one another of mercy after great trials, witnesses of hope in a closed horizon. We had to interrupt our brief dialogue with the feeling that we would not be able to finish it.

I do not know which one of us ended the conversation, but I had the last word. When Fr. Alexander proposed that we meet again, I said something like this to him, "Oh, we will see each other again in heaven." I had such a strong impression that the Word we both announced dwelled in his life, more so than in mine, and that his life was inevitably to become the sign of that Word.

When I heard of Fr. Alexander's death, I had buried this final sentence in my memory. Fr. Men brought it to my mind, after his death. Here is how.

Thanks to Andrei Eriomin, the details of our conversation were reported. Eriomin, a Russian intellectual, had been an acolyte at Novaya Derevnia for some ten years, and for a certain time had functioned as Fr. Alexander's secretary. After our departure from Novaya Derevnia, Fr. Alexander spoke to Andrei Eriomin in more or less the following words:

I just had a striking conversation with Cardinal Lustiger. He told me that we could not talk very much because we were surrounded by people listening to us. The Cardinal said that he was very happy to have met me and added, "We no doubt will not have the occasion to meet again, and we will only see each other in the Beyond."

After Fr. Alexander's death, Andrei Eriomin came to see me on Feb. 1, 1992, to ask me what I had meant and why I had made that statement. In truth, I made it because I saw Fr. Alexander's life as an offering and as an abandonment to the love of Christ, the source of all his courage. I did not prophesy his death. I said out loud only what Fr. Alexander already knew through Jesus' words to Peter: "...and another will gird you and carry you where you do not wish to go." (John 21:18)

I consider my short meeting with Fr. Alexander to have been a grace from God; it was an anticipation of the fullness to come, a fullness that, though it is a future reality, is nonetheless partially present here and now.

Cardinal Jean-Marie Lustiger

Footnotes

(Dates are listed following the system of the French original.
Thus a publication date of 03/01/89 indicates
January 3, 1989, not March 1.)

1   Cited by Andrey Yeromin in his manuscript Pobezhday zlo dobrom (see footnote 239).

2   Originally the Preface to the Russian-language edition.

3   Here Archbishop MIKHAIL is suggesting that the ministry of evangelism will have a transforming effect on all aspects of the Orthdox Church's ministry.

4   "Not distinguished by its 'adequacy'"refers to the world's inability to receive the Gospel message.

5   Russian names are expressed in an admittedly inconsistent manner in this book. While transliteration has been preferred, some names are already familiar in anglicized forms: hence Alexander Men (not Aleksandr Men'), St. Sergius (not Sergei), etc. -editor.

6   Ogonyok, #39, 1990.

7   Zemshchina, #13, May 1991.

8   Tatiana Glinka, "Tsvety u dorogi" [Flowers on the Side of the Road], Moskovskaya pravda, Nov. 11, 1990.

9   Mt 27:43.

10 Protoirei Alexandr Men, "Dorozhite vremenem" [Save Your Time], Svet vo tme svetit [The Light Shines in the Darkness], Moscow, 1991, p. 197

11 "Vladimir Levi ob Aleksandre Mene, 'Prikhodilo zhivoe schastie' [Vladimir Levi Speaks About Alexander Men: It Was Living Happiness That Arrived], Stolitsa, #31-32, 1991.

12 Ibid.

[13] Zoya Maslennikova, "Fenomen o. Aleksandra Menia" [The Phenomenon of Fr. Alexander Men], Perspektivy, #4, 1991, p.55

[14] Andrei Bessmertny and Vladimir Oivin, "On byl golosom istiny v nashe vremia" [He was the Voice of Truth in Our Time], Protestant, Oct. 1990.

[15] L. I. Vassilenko, "Kultura, tserkovnoe sluzhenie I svyatost" [Culture, the Service of the Church, and Holiness], Aequinox, Moscow, 1991, p. 174

[16] In the Arbat section, in front of St. Simeon's church, today on Kalinin Street.

[17] Andre Gide, Retour de l'URSS [Return from the USSR], Gallimard, 1936, p. 15.

[18] Ibid, p.110

[19] The astonishing succession of startsy at Optina was an event unique in the history of Russia. The spiritual guidance of laypeople by experienced monks was by no means something new, however, as the Desert Fathers of the fourth century bear witness. Much of St. Seraphim's spiritual teaching has been preserved thanks to one of his spiritual children, the layman Motovilov. Likewise the original title of the 19th century book known to English speakers as "The Way of a Pilgrim" is: "Confessions of a Pilgrim to His Spiritual Father". -editor..

[20] Ivan Kologrivof, Essai sur la saintete russe [An Essay on Russian Holiness], Editions Beyaert, Bruges, 1953, p. 414

[21] Vassily Bellavin in the world (1865-1925). In the Orthodox Church, monks (and bishops, who are chosen from among the monks) receive a new name when they take their vows. The monk's baptismal and family names are ordinarily no longer used. In this book, the civil names of monks and hierarchs will be indicated by footnote when necessary.

[22] K. Marx, Critique of the Hegelian Philosophy of Law, 1844.

[23] Lenin's Letters to Gorky from November to December 1913.

[24] N. Bukharin and E. Preobrazhensky, ABC du communisme [The ABC's of Communism], Petite collection Maspero, vol. 2, 1971, p. 85

25 The secret letter was addressed by Lenin to the Politburo on November 19, 1922. Le messager orthodoxe, #52, 1970, Paris, pp. 62-65. In Russia, this text was first published only in 1990.

26 The Orthodox tradition is not opposed to married bishops in principle. Some apostles and bishops of the early Church were married. Widowers can also be bishops. There is nowadays a growing movement to restore a married episcopate. -translator.

27 Ivan Stragorodsky in the world, 1867-1925.

28 Her maiden name was Zupersein.

29 Her family name was Vassilevskaya.

30 Elena Semenovna Men, "Moi Put'" [My Path] in I bylo utro, [There Was a Morning: Memories of Fr. Alexander Men], Vita-Tsentr, Moscow, 1992, pp. 155ff.

31 Vera Vassilevskaya, "Fragmenty iz knigi Katakomby XX veka [Extracts from the Book The Catacombs of the 20th Century] in I bylo utro..., ibid., p. 67. Other works of Vera Vassilevskaya have been published under the title: "Dva portreta" [Two Portraits] in the journal Vestnik RkhD, #142, 1978, Paris, pp. 269-298, and in the collection Pamyat, Istoricheskii sbornik [Memory: an Historical Collection], vol. 2, YMCA-Press, Paris, 1979, pp. 481-512

32 In 1953 the street was renamed Bogdan Khemelnitsky Street.

33 This church was destroyed in the beginning of the 1930's.

34 In the world, Sergius Batiukov (1880-1942)

35 In the world, Sergei Sakharov (1887-1942). On the life of Bishop Afanassy, see "Krestny put' preosvyashchennogo Afanassia Sakharova" [The Way of the Cross of Bishop Afanassy Sakharov], Vestnik RSKhD, #107, 1973, pp. 170-211 and "NVT, Episkop Afanassii (Sakharov)," Vestnik RSKhD, #139, 1983, pp. 195-217.

36 Marina Vekhova, "Vseistselyaiushchee slovo" [The All-healing Word], in Pamyati protoiereya Alexandra Menia [In Memory of Archpriest Alexander Men], Moscow, 1991, p. 189.

[37] Izba: one of the wooden houses typical of the Russian countryside. - editor.

[38] "Dva Portreta", in Pamyat, (note 24), p. 489.

[39] Note 22.

[40] Prot. A. Men, "Pismo k E. N." [Letter to E. N.] in Aequinox, (note 10), p. 184.

[41] In the world, Ivan Botcharov (1880-1959).

[42] Piotr Shipkov (1881-1959).

[43] It seems her name was Ksenia Grishanova.

[44] Mt. 26:31.

[45] at 28 Dustarnya Street.

[46] Men, "Pismo...", (note 32), pp. 184-185.

[47] In the world, Sergei Simansky (1877-1970).

[48] the dvatsatka, or "group of twenty".

[49] Episkop Afanassii Kovrovsky, "Mozhno li poseshchat' khramy Moskovskoi patriarkhii?"[Can we Go to the Churches of the Moscow Patriarchate?], Vestnik RSKhD,106, 1972, pp. 92-97.

[50] "Dva portreta," Pamyat, (note 24), p. 503.

[51] Ibid.

[52] This name must not be confused with that of Fr. Alexander's cousin.

[53] A. Zorin, "Angel Chernorabochii", Nezavisimaya gazeta, 10/09/1991.

[54] at 38 Bolshaya Serpukhovka Street.

[55] M. Vekhova, "Vseistselyaiushchee slovo"", p. 190.

56 Located just in front of the Plekhanov Economic Institute on Stremianny Pereulok Street.

57 "First theology"

58 Z. Maslennikova, "Fenomen o. Aleksandra Menia," Perspektivy,#4, p. 46.

59 Aleksandr Belavin, "Svyashchennik Aleksandr Men" [The Priest Alexander Men], Pamyati protoiereia Aleksandra Menia, p. 29

60 An interview by Irina Bystrova, Moskovsky komsomolets 24/05/1989.

61 Vassilenko, (note 10), p. 166

62 Men, "Pismo...," (note 32), p. 185.

63 Nicholas Berdyaev (1874-1948) and Sergius Bulgakov (1871-1944) lived in Paris after their expulsion. Fr. Alexander also cited other Russian thinkers who had influenced him: Simon Frank, who was born in Moscow in 1877 and died in England in 1950; Nicholas Lossky, born in Russia in 1870 and died in France in 1965; Eugene Trubetskoy (1863-1920); and Fr. Florensky, who was born in 1882 and died in the gulag at an unknown date.

64 Alexis Khomiakov (1804-1860).

65 from an unedited autobiography addressed to the author in 1984.

66 Vladimir Soloviev (1853-1900).

67 See F. Rouleau, "Introduction to Vladimir Soloviev," La Sophia et autres ecrits francais [Sophia and other French Writings], Lausanne, L'Age d'Homme, 1978, p. X.

68 Vassilenko, (note 10), p. 171.

69 I bid., p. 170.

70 "Angel chernorabochii," Nezavisimaya gazeta, 10/09/1991.

71 An interview by Irina Bystrova, Moskovsky komsomolets 24/05/1989.

72 Men, "Pismo...," (note 32), p. 185.

[73] In the Krasnaya Presnia district, Maly Predtechensky Pereulok Street.

[74] In the world, Kyrill Vakhromeev. See Pamyati, (note 500, p. 264.

[75] Z. Maslennikova, "Fenomen o. Aleksandra Menia," Perspektivy, #4, p. 48.

[76] An unedited autobiography addressed to the author in 1984.

[77] 1900-1963. He served the parish of the Deposition of the Virgin's Veil, Donskaya Street.

[78] Men, "Pismo...," (note 32), pp. 185-186.

[79] Bishop Palladii. In the world, Pavel Sherstennikov (1898-1976).

[80] A. E. Levitin-Krasnov, V poiskakh novogo grada[In Search of a Nw City], Tel-Aviv, 1980, pp. 225-226.

[81] Nadia Mandelstam, Contre tout espoir [Against All Hope], Paris, Gallimard, 1972, p. 344.

[82] A. Solzhenitsyn, Cancer Ward, ch. 31.

[83] "Dva portreta", (note 24), pp. 504-508.

[84] "Compte rendu d'une conference du president du Conseil aux affaires religieuses aupres du Conseil des ministres de l'URSS," [Minutes of a Conference by the President of the Council on Religious Affairs for the Council of Ministers of the USSR], La documentation catholique #1964, 19/06/1988, p. 641.

[85] For the details of this anti-religious offensive, see N. Struve, Les chretiens en URSS, [Christians in the USSR], 1964, pp. 255 ff.

[86] Rapport secret au Comite central sur l'etat de l'Eglise en URSS [A Secret Report to the Central Committee on the State of the Church in the USSR], Paris, Seuil, 1980, p. 151.

[87] In the world, Boris Yarushevich (1892-1961).

[88] Levitin-Krasnov, (note 71), pp. 132-146.

[89] In the world, Alexei Golubev (1896-1978).

90 Vestnik RkhD, #116, 1975, p. 228.

91 Anatoli Levitin (1914-1991). He wrote in the samizdat press under the pseudonym Krasnov.

92 Sergei Zheludkov (1909-1984).

93 Andrei Siniavsky now lives in France and publishes sometimes under his own name, sometimes under the pseudonym Abram Tertz.

94 Svetlana Alliluyeva, En une seule annee [In a Single Year], Robert Laffont, 1970, pp. 255-261.

95 Bishop Makary, then Archbishop of Mozhaisk. His name in the world was Sergei Daev (1888-1960).

96 This was the church of the Protection of the Virgin in the village of Akulovo, southwest of Moscow, a few miles north of the Vnukovo Airport on the railroad line starting from the Byelorussian Station.

97 Bishop Stephan, in the world Sergei Nikitin (1895-1963). Before becoming a monk he had been a doctor, and close to the community of the Frs. Mechev.

98 Located in the southwest part of Moscow, about thirty miles from the center, on the railroad line starting from Kiev Station, just before getting to Naro-Fominsk. The church here is also named for the Protection of the Virgin.

99 President.

100 A Sukhikh and L. Bondarenko, "Sovremennoe pravoslavie I doistvennaya istina" [Contemporary Orthodoxy and Two-faced Truth], Nauka I religiya #3, 1964, p. 14.

101 Fr. Sergei Khokhlov.

102 In Russia, a modest stipend is often given for this service. Such readers are often enrolled in the lesser ranks of the clergy. -editor.

103 Alexei Trushin.

104 1964.

105 The commemoration is on August 15. The date, as computed by the Julian Calendar in use by the Russian and many other Orthodox Churches, corresponds to August 28th on the civil calendar. The same 13-day discrepancy holds for all fixed feasts.

106 In the metropolitan area of Sherkizovo.

107 For these portraits, see Levitin-Krasnov (note 71), pp. 221-227, 233-237, and 230.

108 Then bishop of Kaluga.

109 Struve, (note 76), p. 266.

110 hese letters are found in Gleb Yakunin, Un pretre seul au pays des Soviets [A Priest Alone in the Land of the Soviets], Criterion, 1984. The function of head of State was then carried out by Podgorny, who, as president of the Presidium of the Supreme Soviet of the USSR, was only a figurehead. The real power belonged to the general secretary of the party, Leonid Brezhnev.

111 Solzhenitsyn, Le chene et le veau [The Oak and the Calf], Paris, Seuil, 1975, p. 152.

112 On the letter of Frs. Yakunin and Eschliman, see Arkadiev, "Neskolko slov o dele dvukh moskovskikh svyashchennikov" [Some Words on the Affair of the Two Moscow Priests], Vestnik RkhD, #95-96, 1970, pp. 99-106. This article was very likely written by Fr. Alexander to plead the cause of Frs. Yakunin and Eschliman. When Patriarch Alexis I died in 1970, it was hoped that the council called to elect a successor would lift the sanction issued by the dead patriarch against them.

113 Mt. 9:37.

114 da Samizt literally means "self-published"; tamizdat, "published over there", i.e., abroad. -editor.

115 N. Struve, "L'homme sovietique soixante ans apres" [The Soviet Man Sixty Years After], Commentaire #14, summer 1981, p.233.

116 G. Orwell, Nineteen Eighty-Four, London, Secker and Warburg, 1966, p. 220.

[117] On this question, see Tatiana Goricheva, Nous, convertis d'Union sovietique [We Converts of the Soviet Union], Nouvelle Cite, 1983, pp. 119-121.

[118] To make this procedure easier, a new article was introduced into the penal code, which had been liberalized under Khrushchev; it imposed a one to three-year sentence in the gulag for anyone guilty of the "systematic spreading", either oral or written, "of blatantly false statements that denigrate the political and social system of the Soviet Union."

[119] To make this procedure easier, a new article was introduced into the penal code, which had been liberalized under Khrushchev; it imposed a one to three-year sentence in the gulag for anyone guilty of the "systematic spreading", either oral or written, "of blatantly false statements that denigrate the political and social system of the Soviet Union."

[120] A. Solzhenitsyn, Bodalsya telenok s dubom, YMCA-Press, Paris, 1975, p. 295.

[121] ibid., p. 395.

[122] S. Adachev, "Nivy pobeleli" [The Fields have Whitened], a text that circulated in the samizdat press.

[123] Vestnik RSKhD, #95-96, 1970, p. 80.

[124] Komsomolskaya Pravda, 16/10/1970.

[125] Adachev, (note 107).

[126] Hieromonk Innokenty (S.N. Pavlov), "O sovremennom sostoyanii russkoi pravoslavnoi Tserkvi"[On the Present State of the Russian Orthodox Church], Sotsiologicheskie isledovania, #4, 1987, pp. 39-40.

[127] Vladimir Zielinsky, "Ceux qui entrent dans l'Eglise, Une nouvelle generation de croyants" [Those Who are Entering the Church: A New Generation of Believers], Histoire de l'Eglise russe, Nouvelle Cite, 1989, pp. 241-242.

[128] Members of the KGB.

[129] A.E. Levitin-Krasnov, "O polozhenii russkoi pravoslavnoi Tserkvi" [On the State of the Russian Orthodox Church], Vestnik RSKhD, #95-96, 1970, p. 81

[130] Goricheva (note 103), p. 25.

[131] Svyashchennik Georgi Edelstein, "Iz zapisok sovetskogo svyashchennika" [Excerpts From the Notes of a Soviet Priest], Na puti k svobode sovesti [On the Road to Freedom of Conscience], Progress, Moscow, 1989, pp. 241-242.

[132] Jacques Loew, Le bonheur d'etre homme [The Happiness of being Man], Centurion, 1988, pp. 290-291.

[133] Levitin-Krasnov, (note 71), pp. 237-238.

[134] Fr. Vladimir Smirnov (1903-1981).

[135] Olga Nikolaevna Vysheslavtseva.

[136] Levitin-Krasnov, (note 71), p. 195.

[137] Fr. Alipy, who died in 1975.

[138] In the world, Tikhon Botozsky (1898-1978). See the very evocative portrait in Zielinsky, (note 112), pp. 195-200.   Editor's note: the English-published Orthodox journal Sourozh has featured several articles dedicated to him. See its issues #9 (August '82), 11 and 12 (February and May of '83, respectively).

[139] Statement by Sandr Riga during a conference in Riga, May 1989. See Prizyv (a photocopied magazine), #31, 1989, p. 35

[140] Ogorodnikov was joined in the creation of this Seminar by several other dedicated and talented Orthodox Christians, including Lev Regelson, Vladimir Poresh, Tatiana Shchipkova et al. Nor was the Moscow Seminar entirely unique. On this subject see Talking about God is Dangerous (1986 Crossroad Publishing Company), by Tatiana Goricheva, one of the founders of the Leningrad Seminar -editor.

[141] G.R. Golts, Religiya I zakon [Religion and the Law], Moscow, 1975, p. 16.

[142] After the death of Alexis I, a local council of the Russian Orthodox Church met in Zagorsk in 1971, electing Bishop Pimen the new Patriarch. His name in the world was Sergei Izvekov (1910-1990).

[143] The jurisdiction of the Metropolitan of Krutitsy extends over the whole diocese of Moscow, with the exception of the city itself, which is administered by the Patriarch directly.

[144] Glinka, (note 3).

[145] "Vladimir Levi..." (Note 6).

[146] Celebrated on Feb. 2/15 in Russia. The feast is also known by Roman Catholics as the feast of the Purification of the B.V.M.

[147] Andrei Eriomin, "Ty ne uznal vremeni poseshchenia tvoego" [You did not Know the Time of your Visitation], Pamyati (note 29), p. 60.

[148] Vassilenko, (note 10), p. 166.

[149] Eriomin, (note 128), p. 53.

[150] Easter

[151] In the apostolic exhortation of 1975, Evangelii nuntiandi, p. 58, Paul VI set out the charter of base communities for the Catholic Church, directing that they should be "firmly attached to the local Church in which they are grounded." See Jacques Loew, Vous serez mes disciples [You will be my Disciples], Fayard-Mame, pp. 157-159.

[152] V. Fainberg, "Otets Aleksandr, Aleksandr Vladimirovich, Sasha," Pamyati, (note 29), p. 214.

[153] Mk 6:6.

[154] Prot. A. Men, Tainstvo, slovo I obraz [Sacrament, Word, and Image], Brussels, 1980, pp. 165-166.

[155] Ibid, p. 203.

[156] Fainberg, (note 132), pp. 216-217.

[157] M. Vekhova, "Vseistselyaiushchee slovo", Pamyati (note 29), pp. 187-188.

[158] Belavin, (note 50), p. 31.

[159] Eriomin, (note 128), pp. 49 & 51.

[160] Hosea 6:6, Mt. 9:13 and 12:27.

[161] Men, Tainstvo..., (note 134), p. 203.

[162] Ibid, p. 204.

[163] "Vladimir Levi...",(note 6)..

[164] This text circulated anonymously in samizdat; an English translation appears in Sourozh #5, published in August, 1981. -editor.

[165] Ibid.

[166] Men, "Dorozhite...," (note 5), p. 198.

[167] V. Zelinski, "Slova proshchania" [Words of Farewell], Russkaya mysl, Paris, 14/09/1990.

[168] Solzhenitsyn refers to Fr. Alexander in a supplement to his book The Oak and the Calf, in a series of chapters entitled "The Invisible Ones", that were dedicated to people who had helped him in his struggle in Russia. In order not to compromise these people, Solzhenitsyn waited until now to publish this text. A. Solzhenitsyn, Les Invisibles, Fayard, 1992, p. 215.

[169] Osip Emilyevich Mandelstam (1891-1938) -editor.

[170] Osip Emilyevich Mandelstam (1891-1938) -editor.

[171] See note 72.

[172] "Vladimir Levi...", (note 6).

[173] "Khristianstvo" [Christianity], Russkaya mysl, Paris, #3850, 19/10/1990.

[174] O. Stepurko, "Ty -zhivoi." [You are Alive], in Pamyati (note 29), p. 168.

[175] A. Maslennikova, "K istorii knigi o. Aleksandra Menia 'Syn chelovecheski'"[On the Writing of the Book 'The Son of Man'],

Aequinox (note 10), p. 178.

176 "Khristianstvo" (note 150).

177 Ibid.

178 Vladimir Soloviev, Le developpement dogmatique de l'Eglise [The Dogmatic Development of the Church], Paris, Desclee de Brouwer, 1991, p. 73.

179 "Khristianstvo" (note 150).

180 "Pochemu mne trudno poverit v Boga? Otets Aleksandr otvechaet na nashi voprosy" [Why is it Difficult for Me to Believe in God? Fr. Alexander Answers Our Questions], Rossiya, 16-17/09/1991.

181 1 John 2:15.

182 John 3:16.

183. E. Svetlov, Na poroge Novogo Zaveta [At the Threshold of the New Testament], Brussels, La Vie avec Dieu, 1983, p. 670.

184 Maslennikova, (note 8), pp. 45-46.

185 Men, "Dorozhite..." (Note 5), p. 197.

186 "Pochemu..." (Note 157).

187 He was a representative of the theological current within Protestantism which tried to reinterpret the fundamental dogmas of Christianity in the light of the secularization of contemporary society, a society from which God seemed to be absent. For the Anglican bishop John Robinson, it was not possible to think of God as a personal being "entirely Other than man": the word God meant "the ultimate ground of all our being", while Jesus Christ was "the man for others".

188 John A. T. Robinson (1910-1984) explained his ideas in a book which appeared in 1963, called Honest to God. It became a best-seller and caused great controversy. Afterwards, as with other theologians of secularized religion, he revised his previous positions. In the area of New Testament exegesis, which was his specialty, he advocated dates for the gospels much earlier than those accepted by most contemporary scholars.

[189] "Interviu na sluchai aresta" [Interview to be Published if Arrested], Vestnik RKhD, #159, 1990, p. 304.

[190] Svetlov, (note 160), p. 669.

[191] "Interviu..." (Note 165), p. 305.

[192] Prot. A. Men, "Osnovnye cherty khristianskago mirovozzrenia" [Essential Traits of the Christian World-view], Simvol (Meudon), #21, July 1989, p. 87.

[193] Conversation with the author.

[194] Autobiography (note 56).

[195] "Interviu..." (Note 165), p. 305.

[196] Men, "Osnovnye..." (Note 168), p. 88.

[197] Prot. A. Men, "Prislushatsia k bytiiu" [Lend Your Ear to Being], Za inzhenerny kadry, 134/02/1990.

[198] .Interview by Pilar Bonet, Panorama #13, December 1990.

[199] Ibid.

[200] i.e., outside the border of the (Soviet) Russian republic, and so difficult of access.

[201] Prot. A. Men, "Evrei I khristianstvo" [The Jews and Christianity], Vestnik RKhD, #117, 1976, p. 115.

[202] Interview, #14 (note 174).

[203] "Interviu..." (Note 165), p. 305.

[204] Men, "Evrei..." (Note 176), p. 114.

[205] Ibid, p. 115.

[206] Ibid, p. 117.

[207] Luke 19:44.

[208] "Interviu..." (Note 165), p. 305.

[209] Col. 1:28.

[210] "Interviu..." (Note 165), p. 300.

[211] "Vladimir Levi..." (Note 6).

[212] "Interviu..." (Note 165), p. 300.

[213] Men, "Pis'mo...", (note 32), p. 188.

[214] Russian: Zhizn' c Bogom (Life with God).

[215] Fr. Valent Romensky.

[216] This and similar groups provided real and commendable help to Orthodox Christians in the USSR. However, not all such efforts were entirely altruistic. This book, the work of a French Catholic, understandably reflects a Roman Catholic view of Orthodoxy and its relationship (both real and hoped for) with Catholicism. This view has, in turn, led to some perceptions of the "needs of the Orthodox", and the means of filling them, that are disputed by the Orthodox themselves. On the proselytism of Orthodox Russians by Catholics during the Stalinist era, see: Walter Ciszek, S.J., With God in Russia, Doubleday. -editor.

[217] Thus, two well-known specialists of the anti-religious campaign were very indignant: "Through the will and cooperation of its sponsors, the publishing house "La Vie avec Dieu" is helping to exercise a spiritual influence over the minds of millions of people." Belov and Shilkin, Religiya v sovremennoi ideologicheskoi bor'be [Religion in Today's Ideological Struggle], Moscow, 1971.

[218] A letter to the author.

[219] Solzhenitsyn, Les Invisibles, (note 147), pp. 217-221.

[220] The book was republished in 1980 in a new edition under Fr. Alexander's name, with a new title: Sacrament, Word, and Image.

[221] Svetlov, (note 160), pp. 665-666.

[222] E. Svetlov, Istoki religii [Sources of Religion], Brussels, 1970.

[223] Ibid, p. 20.

[224] E. Svetlov, Magizm I edinobozhie [Magic and Monotheism], Brussels, 1971.

[225] "Na poroge..." (Note 160), pp. 11-12.

[226] E. Svetlov, U vrat mol'chaniya, Brussels, 1971.

[227] E. Svetlov, Dionisi, Logos, Sud'ba, Brussels, 1972.

[228] E. Svetlov, Vestniki Tsarstva Bozhiya, Brussels, 1972.

[229] "Na poroge..." (Note 160).

[230] Ibid, pp. 12-13.

[231] Gal. 4:4.

[232] Prot. A. Men, Kak chitat' Bibliu, Brussels, 1981.

[233] Letter to the author.

[234] A. Pavlov, Otkuda yavilos vsyo eto?, Naples, 1972.

[235] These catechetical workbooks had originally been published by Fetes et saisons in the 1950's: Dieu existe, Le mal, and qui es-tu? etc.

[236] Fr. Onfroy helped the Eastern Center mostly through his newsletter called Notre Dame des temps nouveaux.

[237] Glinka, (note 3).

[238] An interview by I. Bystrova, Moskovski komsomolets 24/05/1989.

[239] Letter to the author, 1980.

[240] "Interviu..." (Note 165), p. 303.

[241] Vestnik RKhD, #117, 1976, pp. 112-117.

[242] Interview by Pilar Bonet, Panorama #13, December 1990.

[243] Vekhova, (note 29), p. 192.

[244] S. Aversintsev, "Vseistselyaiushchee slovo", in Pamyati (note 29), p. 38.

[245] "Vladimir Levi" (note 6).

[246] Stepurko, (note 151), p. 166.

[247] "Vladimir Levi" (note 6).

[248] Letter to the author.

[249] M. Popovski, "Za chto travyat otsa Aleksandra Menia?" [Why is Fr. Alexander Men being Harassed?], Orthodox almanac Put', February, 1984.

[250] Letter to the author.

[251] Described in Chapter Three of this book.

[252] Interview by I. Bystrova (note 51).

[253] Fr. John Meyendorff (1929-1992).

[254] Letter of November 1986.

[255] Born in 1935, and named Vladimir Poyarkov in the world, Juvenaly has been Metropolitan of Krutitsy since 1977.

[256] "Minutes...", (note 75), pp. 640-643.

[257] Nauka I religiya, November 1987.

[258] "Minutes...", (note 75), p. 642.

[259] A. Men, "O Russkoi pravoslavnoi bibleistike" [Concerning Russian Orthodox Biblical Science], Bogoslovskie Trudy [Theological Works], #28, 1987, pp. 272-289.

[260] Roughly the equivalent of military decorations and citations, these nagrady are awarded, usually to clergy, for outstanding or sustained service. The bestowal of an award on Fr. Alexander at this time was an

acknowledgment by his hierarchs that his work had not gone un-noticed or unappreciated. -editor.

[261] Henryk Paprocki, "Taina smerti otsa Aleksandra" [The Mystery of Fr. Alexander's Death], Pamyati (note 29), p. 105.

[262] Belavin, (note 50), p. 33.

[263] Knizhnoe obozrenie [Book Review], 02/09/1988.

[264] Izvestia, 21/10/1988.

[265] Glinka, (note 3).

[266] Fainberg, (note 132), p. 251.

[267] Andrei Eriomin, "Pobezhdai zlo dobrom" [Overcome Evil Through Good]. Quoted here from the manuscript of this article given to the author; it was later published. See note 241 below.

[268] bid.

[269] Belavin, (note 50), p. 33.

[270] Eriomin, "Pobezhdai..." Znamia #9, 1991, p. 181.

[271] A street in Moscow open only to pedestrians where painters sell their works to passers-by.

[272] Fainberg, (note 132), p. 250.

[273] Interview with the Spanish journalist Pilar Bonet, 05/09/1990.

[274] Sermon given on 15/09/1990.

[275] The capital city of the Georgian republic.

[276] Re-translated from the Russian text: "Slovo ob otse Aleksandre Mene" [A Word Concerning Fr. Alexander Men], in Aleksandr Men, Radostnaya Vest' [Joyful News], Moscow, 1991, p. 7.

[277] A. Men, "Po zavetam miloserdia" [At Mercy's Behest], Moskovski komsomolets, 10/06/1990.

[278] "Slovo poiznessennoe pered otpevaniem protoierea Aleksandra Menia" [Address spoken before the funeral of Archpriest Alexander Men], Pamyati (note 29), p. 21.

[279] Interview (note 243).

[280] Literally: les nostalgiques.

[281] Moskovskie novosti [Moscow News], 20/09/1987.

[282] Interview, (note 243).

[283] Natalia Bolshakova, "Posledni den" [The Last Day], Khristianos (Riga), #1, 1991, p.16.

[284] Based on the witness of Sergei Gussev in a program broadcast on Soviet television commemorating the fourth anniversary of Fr. Alexander's death.

[285] Fr. Daniel Ange, "Hommage a un martyr" [Homage to a martyr], Famille chretienne, 04/10/1990.

[286] The contemporary Russian expression for the Brezhnev era.

[287] The popular name for the early twentieth-century, reactionary Union of the Russian People, and henceforth a synonym for the militant, extreme right. -editor.

[288] "Vladimir Levi", (note 6).

[289] Fainberg, (note 132), p. 250.

Photograph Credits

Publisher's Note

We are honored to have the opportunity to publish this definitive biography of a modern martyr, witness and evangelist of the Orthodox Faith. During 1995-96, we will further publish the works of Fr. Men himself, including:

CONVERSATIONS CONCERNING THE CHURCH AND THE FAITH
THE SON OF MAN

Other Books By Oakwood Publications

AN ICONOGRAPHER'S SKETCHBOOK VOLUME 1:
  THE POSTNIKOV COLLECTION (MELNICK):
AN ICONOGRAPHER'S SKETCHBOOK VOLUME 2:
  THE TYULIN COLLECTION (MELNICK)
AN ICON PAINTER'S NOTEBOOK: THE BOLSHAKOV EDITION (MELNICK)
THE IMAGE OF GOD THE FATHER IN ORTHODOX THEOLOGY AND ICONOGRAPHY AND OTHER STUDIES (BIGHAM)
ORTHODOX FATHERS, ORTHODOX FAITH (AL-KHOURY)

OF PREACHING IN AMERICA (AL-KHOURY)
THE ILLUMINATED GOSPEL OF ST. MATTHEW (ANDREJEV)
AN ICONOGRAPHER'S PATTERNBOOK: THE STROGANOV TRADITION (KELLEY)
THE PAINTER'S MANUAL OF DIONYSIUS OF FOURNA (HETHERINGTON)   THE ICON: IMAGE OF THE INVISIBLE: ELEMENTS OF THEOLOGY, AESTHETICS & TECHNIQUE (SENDLER)
THE ART OF THE ICON: A THEOLOGY OF BEAUTY (EVDOKIMOV)
ICON COLLECTIONS IN THE UNITED STATES (BARNS)
DYNAMIC SYMMETRY PROPORTIONAL SYSTEMS IN ICONS (KNEE)
ICONS & ICONPAINTING (VIDEOTAPE) (BELL)
THE MINISTRY OF WOMEN IN THE CHURCH (BEHR-SIGEL)
THE PLACE OF THE HEART: AN INTRODUCTION TO ORTHODOX   SPIRITUALITY (BEHR-SIGEL)